Human Resource Management in Local Government

Managing Local Government Series

Human Resource Management in Local Government

its special purposes, conditions and tasks

by Alan Fowler

General Editors:
Michael Clarke and John Stewart

Second Edition

in association with the Institute of Local Government Studies

PITMAN PUBLISHING
128 Long Acre, London WC2E 9AN

A division of Pearson Professional Limited

First published in Great Britain 1988

First edition © Longman Group UK Ltd 1988
Second edition © Pearson Professional Limited 1995

British Library Cataloguing in Publication Data
A CIP catalogue record for this book can be obtained from the British Library.

ISBN 0 273 61933 0 (2nd edition)

ISBN 0 582 02554 0 (1st edition)

10 9 8 7 6 5 4 3 2 1

Typeset by Phoenix Photosetting, Chatham, Kent
Printed by Bell and Bain Ltd., Glasgow

The Publishers' policy is to use paper manufactured from sustainable forests.

Contents

Editors' foreword to the second edition

This book is one of a series of management handbooks published by Pitman Publishing in association with the Institute of Local Government Studies in the School of Public Policy at the University of Birmingham. The series is designed to help those concerned with management in local government to meet the challenge of the late 1990s. It is based on the belief that no period has been so important for local authorities to have effective management, responsive to both citizen and customer.

The mid 1990s has brought reorganisation to local authorities in Scotland, Wales and parts of England. No local authority, however, can escape the need to keep under continuous review its political and managerial structures and processes. All councils are caught up in far-reaching changes. Some of these come from local determination and decision, others from central government policy and yet others from deeper changes in society. New problems, issues and opportunities demand from local governments a capacity to respond in new ways. They have to become closer to their local communities, their public and the wide range of institutions and organisations involved in the governance of localities; they need to find imaginative solutions to the evermore complex problems of public policy; they have to manage their resources to achieve value for money and value in the services they provide; and they have to achieve effective management in all their activities. These are formidable challenges for the managers—and the politicians—involved.

There are plenty of management books, but this series is distinct. Its starting point is the need for emphasis on developing effective management in local government, associated with the need to take account of the particular nature of local government. The series sets out to be succinct and to be useful in the practical day-to-day world as well as being designed to be used as a prompt to management improvement.

In no sense are we pretending that this or other books in the series will show a *one right way* to manage the local authority. Management is not like that. Our intention is to explore ideas and questions in order to help fashion the most helpful and effective approach to the local situation. We believe that local authority politicians and managers should draw on as wide a range of experience as possible but that this should be set in the context of the special purposes, conditions and tasks of local government. We hope that this book contributes to that end.

Professor Michael Clarke, Head of School of Public Policy
University of Birmingham

Professor John Stewart, Institute of Local Government Studies
School of Public Policy, University of Birmingham

Introduction

Management literature tends to fall into two categories—books for line managers about general management principles, and texts dealing with specific functions, written for specialists. There are certainly many publications about personnel management which are aimed mostly at the personnel manager or personnel management student.

Yet personnel specialists have executive authority for managing directly only the very small numbers of staff in their own departments. The effective management of people is a central function of all managers so that effective personnel management is neither more nor less than effective general management.

If I were asked to describe this book in a single phrase it would be 'personnel management for line managers'. It should, of course, also be of interest to personnel specialists—even if only to discover what their line managers are being told to expect from the personnel function! But the book's main objective is to provide information and ideas about the effective management of people to managers, general or specialist, whose jobs involve getting things done through their employees—in other words, all managers.

The terminology 'human resource management' has been used not because it is fashionable (it is) or elegant (it isn't) but because it emphasises the concept of people as a resource rather than a cost—as a capital asset rather than as revenue expenditure.

The text includes many examples of local authority practice and some material drawn from other sectors. In general, I have not identified the authorities concerned and for two reasons. First, I have included some examples of bad practice (we can all learn from mistakes) and it would not be fair to name authorities which by now may well have changed their ways. Secondly, I have noticed a tendency for named examples to be discounted. Some authorities become stereotyped (often inaccurately) and anything they do is then set aside as 'typical Bogshire'. But there are lessons to be learned from an intelligent use of cases and comparisons, and this can be encouraged by concentrating on what authorities do, rather than on who they are.

I have been aided by having access to a wide range of information and comment, formal and informal, from many local government and other sources. Following the policy of anonymity, I have not been able within the text to identify and acknowledge all this help. Instead, I am using this introduction to thank all those who have contributed, wittingly or otherwise. Without their help, this book could not have been written and I am extremely grateful for their assistance.

In addition to information obtained directly from local authorities, I have also been aided considerably by material drawn from the *Local Government Management Board, Society of Chief Personnel Officers, the Institute of Personnel and Development, South East Employers' Organisation* and the *Audit Commission*. My grateful thanks are due to all the officers of these organisations who have provided me with such ready assistance.

Alan Fowler

1

The importance of people and human resource management

KEY POINTS

- People are the primary resource.

- Personnel policies and practices need to be integrated with the total direction and management of the authority.

- Strategic planning, and a matching of the style of employment practice to the authority's culture, is needed to maximise the effectiveness of the human resource.

- Human resource management is a prime responsibility of all managers, not a specialist role.

The term 'human resource management' as used in this book is not just a form of jargon to describe personnel management. It represents a different approach to the management of people in which the emphasis is placed on the role of the line manager, rather than the specialist; and on strategic, as well as tactical, considerations. It is part of a wider trend in general management thinking which has developed during the 1980s in the USA and the UK, and which derives largely from studies of the common characteristics of successful private and public sector organisations.

These studies indicate that the primary factors leading to success—or 'excellence', to use the key word in the literature—are not organisational structures of any specific shape or the adoption of particular management techniques, but rather the more intangible qualities of an organisation's culture, values and vision. In UK local government, these ideas have been given particular impetus by the Audit Commission. To quote from the introduction of the Commission's Code of Practice:

> *Those organisations in the public and private sectors which have been most successful in securing beneficial change have created an environment that thrives on challenge and change, by managing the following elements in such a way as to reinforce each other.*
>
> Vision: *what the authority is seeking to be or achieve.*
>
> Strategy: *how this vision is to be translated into reality.*
>
> Structure: *the way the authority is organised to implement the strategy.*
>
> Systems: *the way in which the people in the organisation plan, decide, control and monitor day-to-day actions as well as long-term progress.*
>
> Staffing and Skills: *the way in which the critical resource in every authority—people—is acquired, trained, deployed, motivated and rewarded.*
>
> Style: *the 'way we do things' and the way members, officers and employees relate to each other and to those they are there to serve.*

In addition to the emphasis given in this statement to vision, strategy and style, two other points emerge which are particularly germane to the concept of human resource management. First, that structure and systems need to be evolved from, and support, the authority's strategic objectives. There is no one best method of doing things for all authorities: structures and procedures need to be tailor-made to fit the priorities and style of each authority individually. Second, that the skills and attitudes of the authority's employees are central to the effective achievement of its objectives: people are 'the critical resource'.

Human resource management is therefore an approach to the management of people which is based on the following key principles:

- People constitute the resource by which the inanimate factors of finance, land, property and equipment are converted into the delivery of services.

- Policies and practices regarding the management of people need to be integrated with the total process of management.

- Strategies need to be evolved to ensure that the authority can obtain, develop, deploy and retain employees with the requisite skills and attitudes.

- The leadership and motivation of an authority's employees is essentially a responsibility of all its managers, not just a task for personnel specialists.

Each of these points is now considered in more detail.

❏ People—the primary resource

There is a tendency to consider revenue expenditure simply as cost and therefore something to be minimised, while treating capital expenditure as investment and therefore desirable. There is, of course, some financial validity in this view, particularly when an authority is faced with severe revenue restrictions or capping. It does, however, encourage a very negative attitude towards the employment of staff. If employees are perceived primarily as a cost, and not in terms of their essential contribution to the delivery of services, an employment policy can become little more than an attempt to reduce the head count and to keep wages at the lowest possible level. This can be illustrated by the following extracts from one authority's annual report:

> *The Council has always been very conscious of the fact that most local government services are inherently staff intensive and that employment costs consequently represent the largest single element of revenue expenditure. Staffing levels are consequently subject to continual monitoring to ensure that every practicable opportunity is taken to reduce manpower. Despite this, employment costs were higher than budgeted because the Council had to implement the undesirably high pay awards negotiated by the various National Joint Councils ... Every opportunity has been taken to maintain a high level of capital expenditure, with capital receipts being used to the full to supplement the level permitted by the government's capital controls. This year's capital payments are the highest ever achieved by the Council.*

The purpose of quoting this extract is not to suggest that all authorities should spend lavishly on staffing, nor to imply that this particular authority was wrong to give a very high priority to capital expenditure. What the quotation does indicate is that concentration on just the revenue expenditure implications of employing people can lead to a bias towards the negative aspects of employment. It shows, too, how the concept of investment—a view which lies at the heart of this authority's pride in its capital programme—creates a wholly positive attitude to this form of expenditure.

Although for sound accountancy reasons it is obviously not possible formally to classify employee costs as capital payments, managerial attitudes towards employment can nevertheless be altered by thinking of people as a primary resource, and of expenditure on people as investment to secure the highest possible quality of this resource. It requires no complex analysis to show that a local authority's ability to deliver services cost-effectively, and in a way which enhances its local reputation, depends critically on the level of skill and commitment of all its employees. The final stages of service delivery are in the hands of individual employees, often working with little direct supervision, exercising their own judgment and initiative, frequently in direct contact with the public. So at 11.30, say, one Tuesday morning, a typical range of activities will be:

- A receptionist is talking to a distraught woman who has called at her local social services office to seek help with her mentally disturbed teenage son.

- In the nearby library, an assistant is being asked by a student if any books are available about the history of crystallography.

- Outside, the chargehand of a small road-repair team has just had a shopowner complain that access for a pending delivery is being blocked by the siting of a pile of asphalt.

- In the school down the road, the mathematics teacher is explaining the importance of literacy to an unenthusiastic 14-year-old.

- In a nearby office, an accountant is pondering on ways and means of helping the Fire Service acquire replacement sets of breathing apparatus while still keeping within their budgeted level of capital payments.

- A district council maintenance worker who is replacing a broken window has just discovered that the window frame is rotten.

- At the district's environmental health office, a caller is demanding immediate action to deal with smells emanating from a newly-opened food-processing factory on the town outskirts.

In these examples, consider the different outcomes which are likely from two different kinds of workforce. The first is well-trained and highly motivated; the second has low morale and inadequate skills. It takes little imagination to see that in the former case, good decisions will be made and the members of the public concerned will be dealt with courteously and efficiently. In the latter instance, the public will probably be treated brusquely and unhelpfully, and decisions will be taken with the primary aim of avoiding anything that smacks of hard work.

The woman in the social services office will be sent away with a form to fill in. The student will be told that no relevant books are in stock. The shopowner will be told that his problem is nothing to do with the road gang. The teacher will give up trying to explain and imply that the lad is stupid. The accountant will stick to the book and say that the Fire Service cannot be helped. The rotten window frame will go unreported. The caller worried about smells will be told to put her complaint in writing.

Securing a skilled, committed and enthusiastic workforce is far more than a simple matter of recruitment. It can never be taken for granted: it never just happens. It requires a high level of managerial effort and expertise. It is in this sense that expenditure on employees can be seen as investment rather than cost—a view which is particularly relevant to expenditure on training. The negatively minded authority will view training costs simply as an overhead, and in times of financial stringency will readily cut the training budget. The authority which fully recognises the extent to which the effective delivery of its services depends on the quality of its workforce will view training expenditure as an essential investment in its primary resource.

While training is perhaps the most obvious element of this investment approach, other factors are also important. It is difficult, for example, to maintain a high degree of employee commitment if employees feel a deep sense of grievance about their level of pay. Adequate or even high pay will not of itself guarantee high morale—enthusiasm and loyalty cannot just be bought—but inequitable pay systems will demotivate.

But the investment approach goes beyond expenditure. What human resource management requires is the investment by all managers of interest, time and effort in developing their employees' skills and creating the motivational climate in which employees will, with enthusiasm, give of their best.

❏ The integration of personnel and service objectives

If many aspects of managing people are thought of as specialist functions, lying outside the mainstream of general or line management, they may be handled in ways which conflict with (or at least fail to promote) service objectives.

One simple example is the definition of conditions of service relating to work done outside normal office hours, when set against the functions of libraries and leisure centres. The ideal service objective is for these facilities to be open and fully staffed when most of the public are at leisure, i.e. in the evenings, weekends and at bank holidays. However, the conditions of service negotiated by the various National Joint Councils have conventionally imposed very heavy cost penalties on anything other than Monday to Friday, 9–5 working arrangements.

The whole field of conditions of service has been riddled with instances of this kind, in which the evolution of particular rules and procedures has taken place separately from any analysis of service priorities and purposes. In the broadest sense, the overriding objective of all local authority services is the meeting of individual and community needs. How often do industrial relations negotiators test the likely impact of the various options they are considering on this objective? The dynamics of the negotiation process, particularly when only specialist personnel and trade-union practitioners are involved, have tended to lead to the conclusion of an agreement becoming an end in itself—rather than these agreements being tested for their compatibility with service needs and priorities. The need for more flexibility in national agreements, to provide individual authorities with some scope for matching conditions of service to local operational needs, was recognised, however, in the 1987 manual worker pay negotiations.

Since then, there have been further moves towards introducing greater flexibility into conditions of service prescribed by national agreements for both manual and white collar staff. The declared long-term intention of the national employers is to use these agreements simply to set minimum standards for a small number of primary conditions, allowing authorities at local level a large measure of flexibility—both in the local application of national agreements and in the freedom to design their own supplementary local conditions.

Three developments during the late 1980s and into the 1990s have also led to the adoption of an approach to pay and conditions which reflects operational and service aims and realities:

■ To remain competitive under CCT (compulsory competitive tendering), many authorities have found it necessary to change or abandon detailed national prescriptions for conditions such as overtime and shift payments. New, local arrangements have been introduced which are far more flexible and less costly.

■ A greater recognition of the need to meet customer needs and expectations, together with the publication of service performance indicators, has also led to the local introduction of conditions which enable facilities such as leisure centres to be fully staffed at evenings and weekends without incurring the high costs of conventional shift and unsocial hours premium payments.

■ There has been a growing recognition of the need for (and value of) the definition of corporate and service objectives and standards. In terms of management processes, this has led to the widespread introduction of performance management systems. The most effective of these systems provide a linkage between the goals aimed for by the authority and services as a whole, and the objectives for individual employees—normally through performance appraisal schemes.

Nevertheless, there is still a tendency to fail to integrate some personnel management activities with corporate or service objectives. Some appraisal schemes, for example, have been introduced without a supporting framework of broader-based performance management, and are perceived by operational managers as something imposed by the personnel profession, rather than as an aid to effective management. A small selection of cases makes the point:

- A training officer develops a new course for staff in residential children's homes while at the same time the Social Services Director is evolving a major programme of homes closures and the transfer of children in care to foster parents. An integrated approach would have resulted in a training priority for new foster parents, and retraining for the displaced staff.

- The personnel officer mounts a recruitment campaign for accountancy trainees among new graduates at universities across the country, while the Employment Strategy Unit has persuaded the local university to run special accountancy courses for unemployed mature students who are now trying to find work with local employers who are willing to change conventional forms of accountant recruitment. An integrated approach would have resulted in a joint recruitment project, involving the finance and personnel departments working with the Employment Strategy Unit.

- A staff appraisal scheme is introduced, in which assessments of employees' performance are required against various specified criteria—output, quality, and so on. A heavy emphasis is given in these criteria to co-operation with management and working relationships with colleagues, but no mention is made of relationships with the public. Quite separately, the Chief Officers Management Group (which does not include the personnel officer) has decided that every service department should make a major effort to become more public service oriented. The integration of personnel with service objectives would have resulted in the appraisal scheme giving a high priority to the quality of staff's contacts with the public.

On a wider scale, the strong influence of a multiplicity of professional institutes and societies on employees' career expectations and on the nature of jobs does not always best serve the values and objectives of individual authorities. By definition, occupational patterns and standards set by outside bodies on a national basis cannot be fully integrated with the development of individual local authorities' policies. Any compatibility is likely to be more coincidental than intentional. This is not to decry the massive contribution which bodies such as the Chartered Institute of Public Finance and Accounting (CIPFA) has made to standards of professional competence. CIPFA more than most also has a splendid record of working with the local authority associations in developing common practices and in collating and publishing useful data in its own professional field.

It is a matter of emphasis and balance. Professional staff are sometimes so committed to promoting the aims and status of their professional bodies that they lose sight of their primary obligation to further the objectives of their employing authorities. Rigid and very traditional entry and membership regulations of some professional institutes have, in the past, restricted local authorities' ability to cast a wide recruitment net and may have conflicted with equal opportunity policies. Much of the professional training supported by authorities has been designed more to meet the examination criteria of professional institutes than the aims and priorities of the authorities themselves. Too great an emphasis on a diversity of separate professional identities also undermines the growing efforts of at least some authorities to create a more corporate working environment in which employees feel a strong sense of common style and purpose across all departments.

By the mid 1990s, this situation had begun to change. The impact of the National Vocational Qualifications' (NVQ's) principles was being seen not only in the emphasis on work-based training for basic grade staff, but also in the development and assessment of work-oriented competences at the professional level. Most professional institutes by 1995, had either revised their qualification criteria in this direction, or were in the process of doing so. The concept of continuing professional development (CPD) had also been adopted by most of these institutes. To retain their institute membership, many professionals now have to provide periodic evidence that they are continuously updating their knowledge—not just by attending short refresher courses, but also by planned learning from work projects and other practical experience. CPD is thus linking professional know-how more closely to the practicalities and needs of the workplace.

Related changes are also taking place in traditional concepts of career progression. The historically rigid distinction between technicians and professionals are being eroded, with training and qualifications now being seen as providing an integrated progression of learning throughout whole careers. At the management level, it is progressively being recognised that it is not essential for professionals to be at the head of largely professional functions. It is generic management skill which is the priority at chief executive and director level, rather than high-level professional expertise. Consequently, there is a growing diversity of professional backgrounds among top managers with chief executives in particular drawn from a variety of functions such as engineering, leisure services and personnel, in addition to the traditional sources of legal and financial services.

An integrated approach to human resource management requires that 'people issues' are treated neither as separate from service issues nor as something to be thought about after service decisions have been made. Because service delivery is achieved through people, questions about their management need to be dealt with as an integral part of the evolution of service plans, not as a bolt-on extra. Only in this way can complete compatibility and support be secured between a definition of what the authority wants to do, and the effect on employee skills and attitudes of the way the human resource is managed.

❏ A strategic approach

The theme of integration leads directly to the third main element of the human resource concept—that its management needs to be set in a strategic framework. Conventionally, a good deal of industrial relations and personnel practice is essentially tactical rather than strategic. It is concerned with the efficient solution of immediate problems, with little regard to long-term trends and with no definition of long-term aims. Two examples will illustrate this.

- In 1995, the Audit Commission published a report, 'Paying the Piper', which included an analysis of trends in white collar employment and pay over the previous eight years. It showed that the numbers of senior staff in local government had increased by 60% in this period, against a 12% increase in junior staff, with the result that the white collar paybill rose twice as fast as the increase in negotiated pay rates. Many authorities were unaware of this trend, though most operated administrative mechanisms for approving individual staff appointments. What appeared to be missing was any link at the strategic level between authorities' general service objectives and any broadly based staff resourcing policies. There was also a concentration on week-to-week detail without this being set in a longer-term strategic framework.

- A large authority fought a claim of sex discrimination by a woman employee. Losing the case at the industrial tribunal, the authority took the case on appeal, first to the Employment Appeal Tribunal and then to the Court of Appeal, losing at every stage and, in consequence, receiving a fair amount of adverse publicity about its employment practices. The same authority was separately promoting its equal opportunity policy. Set in a strategic context, it seems probable that different tactics would have been adopted in the tribunal case in order not to prejudice the wider-ranging employment policy.

Two broad factors are involved in considering human resource management from a strategic viewpoint:

- the need to plan;
- organisational culture.

Planning

The effective management of any service requires a forward view to be taken about its purpose, scale and changing nature. Most services need to examine the trends of demographic change and adopt service strategies which reflect these changes in the size and age distribution of the population. Housing and social services departments will plan to cope with increases in the over-70 age group. Education departments plan school re-organisations against trends in the birth rate. Building and highways departments have had to reshape their activities to cope with competitive tendering. Many authorities have also adopted the concept of 'business planning'—defining the operational objectives and standards of particular services so that week-to-week operational practice contributes to the achievement of stated long-term aims and standards.

Human resource planning needs to be an integral part of this broad-based business or service planning. It is a requirement which goes beyond the conventional and fairly simple process of statistical manpower planning. This merely attempts to quantify the requisite workforce against any similarly quantified projections of service volumes. The wider concept of human resource planning takes account of qualitative as well as quantifiable change—for example, the need to develop a higher level of 'customer consciousness' among all employees—and then defines the action needed to achieve such objectives. The questions to be asked, relative to each service's operational plans, include:

- Are more or fewer staff required, in which categories of skill or occupation?
- If fewer, how are displaced staff to be handled—Redundancy? Redeployment? Retraining?

- If more, what sources are to be used—Internal through retraining? External recruitment? Are the needs achievable within the desired time-scale? If not, the service plan may have to be changed.

- What scale of investment will be necessary in training or recruitment? Again, is this practicable?

- Are changes needed in attitudinal or motivational characteristics, and how are these to be achieved?

- Are the management skills available to lead and control the desired qualitative and quantitative changes? If not, what can be done—Train? Buy in additional expertise? Use consultants?

- What are trade union and staff reactions likely to be to projected change? What action will be necessary to inform and involve these staff interests? And by whom, on what time-scales?

This is not an exhaustive list, but it illustrates two key points. First, that action plans are necessary in many aspects of human resource management if change is to be effected within reasonable time-scales. Changes in the balance of skills, or in employee attitudes, will occur very slowly (if at all), in the absence of a planned campaign. Secondly, there is a potential interaction between service plans and human resource plans—one does not just follow the other. A number of authorities' plans for the rapid expansion of information technology (IT) foundered on a shortage of staff with relevant skills. IT planning—as with any other form of service development—needs to consider human resource realities as an important element in the planning process, and not something which the personnel department tries to deal with after the service plan has been finalised.

Organisational culture

The other main element in a strategic approach requires a view to be taken of the authority's culture—its style or general character. This subject is considered in more detail in Chapter 3. It is sufficient here to note that personnel practices need to fit an authority's style.

Take as an example an authority which wishes to be highly responsive and quickly adaptable to changing community needs. The keynotes of its desired style are flexibility and care. Suppose, however, that in the personnel field it operates a rigid and complex system of establishment control, with very detailed job descriptions and tall, strictly defined organisational hierarchies. It is improbable that it will be able to operate its services in the desired fashion

11

unless it changes its personnel practices to a much more flexible and adaptable mode.

Local authorities differ markedly in character or culture. There is no one preferred style, and it is surely a desirable feature of local democracy that these differences exist. They derive partly from economic, social and regional differences, and partly from differing political philosophies. The interaction between consciously adopted culture and positively constructed employment policies can be illustrated by two politically opposite authorities—Kent County Council and Sheffield City. Kent, when it pursued a Conservative market-oriented approach with a strong emphasis on the individual accountability of senior managers, widened its salary differentials between the lowest and highest paid employees. Sheffield, as a socialist authority with a strong egalitarian concern for social justice, narrowed its salary differentials by low-pay supplements to manual workers. In both cases, pay systems were being used to reinforce the desired culture.

❏ A general management function

The emphasis placed on the integration of personnel and service aims and activities, and on the need for strategic thinking, links with the fourth major theme of human resource management. This is that the management of people is a central function for all managers—not a peripheral activity which is subordinate to the technical or professional content of a particular service, or a specialist activity which can be left to personnel officers. If personnel policies and procedures are to match, influence and reinforce an authority's whole style, strategy and service plans, then line managers from the chief executive down need to take a leading part in evolving these policies and putting them into effect.

As a statement of management theory, there is nothing very new about this. Management textbooks have for years emphasised the responsibility all managers carry for the management of their staff. Yet in practice, in the private and public sectors, many managers at all levels have continued to place more importance on the technical or functional components of their work than on the development and motivation of their employees. To some extent, the growth of the specialist personnel function has unwittingly encouraged this attitude. Unwittingly, because the Institute of Personnel and Development has consistently emphasised the advisory and support role of personnel specialists, and has never encouraged personnel managers to lay claim to the executive management of the human resource. But the fact that personnel departments exist does lead some managers to pay scant attention to the management of their staff until problems arise—and then to call in the personnel officer to sort things out.

Two main influences have led to a change in practice, with an increasing number of top managers in industry and local government devoting a great deal of personal effort and enthusiasm to improving the quality of the management of people:

- Once top managers recognise that the achievement of business or service plans depends critically on the extent to which personnel planning is integrated with the whole management process, they are inevitably drawn into both the planning and implementation functions.

- Managers' attitude have also been influenced by what many managers see as the failure of the more mechanistic management techniques of the 1960s and 1970s. This applies in particular to formal, highly structured systems of management by objectives which were based almost solely on schedules of quantifiable 'key results' and which ignored factors which could not be reduced to statistics.

It is almost as though there has been a rediscovery of the importance of leadership. Managers have discovered over the years that however sophisticated their systems of work planning may be, plans will not be translated into effective reality if the workforce is lacking in skill, bored, suspicious of management, not understanding of the organisation's values and aims, or generally demotivated. Human resource management itself has been described as the discovery of personnel management by chief executives.

While the central role of line managers cannot be over-emphasised, one danger needs to be recognised. This is that effective personal leadership by line managers is not a substitute for well-planned employment policies and practices. What is needed is a partnership between line managers and personnel specialists. The latter should supply the necessary information (e.g. about employment legislation) and techniques (e.g. psychometric testing for employee selection) and contribute from their specialist viewpoint to strategic corporate discussions about service objectives. Line managers should provide the motivational drive to convert plans into action.

Strategy is not an alternative to tactics—it is the framework or direction within which tactical activity should be set. To evolve effective employment strategies and to be effective leaders, managers need to know what tactical tools are available, what external constraints on action may exist, and what are the roles of the various relevant institutions such as the trade unions, the local authority associations, and other national bodies such as LGMB (Local Government Management Board). This blend of strategic and tactical, theory and practice, concepts and facts, general and specialist roles, influences the content of the next eleven chapters.

QUESTIONS ABOUT YOUR OWN AUTHORITY

- Is expenditure on employees considered solely as a cost, or is it recognised as having some of the positive characteristics of investment?

- Do personnel policies and practices contribute positively to the achievement of the authority's objectives?

- Are qualitative and quantitative human resource needs identified, with consequent planned action?

- Do all managers understand and accept their responsibilities for the leadership, motivation and development of their staff?

2

The staffing characteristics of local government

KEY POINTS

- Local government employs a very large but very diverse workforce: over 2 million employees, 45% being part-timers, 60% women, hundreds of different occupations.

- Each local authority is an autonomous employer: conformity to national conditions is voluntary.

- A multiplicity of organisations—associations, trade unions, professional bodies—each have their own aims and values which can inhibit coherence of attitude and objectives within the individual authority.

- This divergence can be reduced by recognition of the unifying theme of public service.

To talk of local government's human resource gives the impression of a homogeneous workforce and may imply, too, the existence of a single unified service. The phrase often used in an industrial relations context to describe the local authority side of the various National Joint Councils—'the national employers'—compounds this wholly inaccurate impression. In reality, there are no national employers: each local authority is, in law and in fact, an autonomous employer. Local government staff are employees only of their own employing authorities, not of some national service. On the employers' side, therefore, the management of the human resource lies with each of the 400 or so individual local authorities, each of which may develop its own particular managerial style or employment philosophy.

Where employees are concerned, the position is even more complex. The main feature of the human resource in local government is its very considerable diversity. It is important to examine this in some detail as there are few aspects of employee management that can be applied without

15

modification across the whole range of employee categories and different services.

❑ Employee categories

Local government employees can be categorised in several ways:

- part-time and full-time;
- male and female;
- occupational groups;
- hierarchical groups.

Local authorities are major employers of part-timers, who account for about 45% of the total workforce. The range of part-time work is also very wide. At one extreme is the evening-class lecturer working no more than two hours per week for, say, ten weeks per year. At the other extreme is the cook in the staff restaurant working 30 hours per week throughout the year. To monitor manpower volumes requires a standard unit which, given these variations in part-time employment, a simple headcount cannot provide. The unit used by most authorities and by the Joint Staffing Watch (a set of annual statistics produced by LGMB is the 'full-time equivalent'. This is normally calculated by calculating the total weekly hours worked by part-timers and dividing this by the standard weekly hours for the particular employee category. Figure 2.1

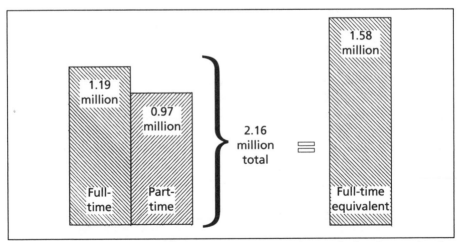

Figure 2.1 Numbers of employees in general services (i.e. excluding law and order services which employ 201,100 full-time and 15,200 part-time)

shows the numbers of full- and part-timers with the full-time equivalent total in 1994. The figures are for what the Joint Staffing Watch describes as general services. These are all local government services in England and Wales except the law and order services of police, magistrates' courts and probation—none of which are wholly under local government control.

Part-time employees are not evenly distributed across all categories and services. Of the nearly one million part-timers, 55% are manual workers and 13% are teachers and lecturers. The education service is a particularly large employer of part-timers, accounting for 47% of the local government total, and with part-time employees (manual, administrative and teaching) forming 42% of the education workforce.

Local government also employs a higher proportion of women than almost any other major employer except the Health Service. As Figure 2.2 shows, over 60% (or some 1.4 million) of the total workforce are women. As it also shows, women employees are heavily concentrated in the part-time category.

One of the most marked features of the local government workforce is the multiplicity of occupations needed to deliver the whole range of local authority services. No comprehensive list of these occupations has ever been compiled, but it must certainly amount to several hundred. In the APT&C

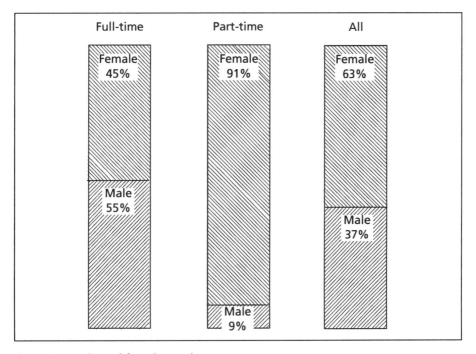

Figure 2.2 Male and female employment

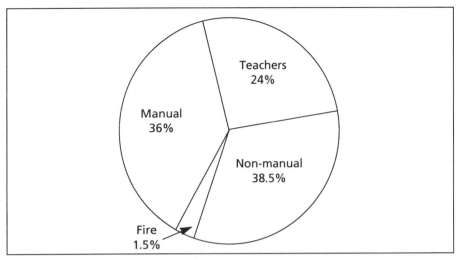

Figure 2.3 Main employee categories

sector (administrative, professional, technical and clerical) it is easy to collect an A to Z of the professions, from architects, say, to zoologists, a few of the latter being employed in environmental conservation teams or in the museum service. One very broad occupational classification is often used in national statistics, and is shown in Figure 2.3. This shows a three-way split between teachers, manuals (including craft) and non-manuals (primarily APT&C) plus a relatively small group of uniformed fire service staff. The percentages are of the raw totals of actual employees, full- and part-time. This gives a slightly misleading picture of real manpower volumes. Recalculated on the basis of full-time equivalents, the percentages change to:

- non-manual, 44%

- manual, 28%

- teachers, 26%

- fire, 2%

Each of the three main groups could be broken down into further detailed occupational categories, though with far more occupations in the manual and non-manual sectors than in the teaching group.

The hierarchical groupings of employees is a feature mainly of the teaching and non-manual categories and is reflected in their salary systems. It is seen at its most marked in the APT&C and chief officers' sector. The number of levels of managers, supervisors and staff in most authorities varies between five and

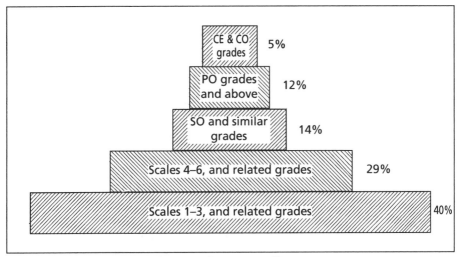

Figure 2.4 Hierarchical distribution of APT&C staff

twelve, with a large number of basic-grade employees at the bottom of a hierarchical pyramid and decreasing numbers at each higher level until the one top post of chief executive is reached. Figure 2.4 shows a simplified grading distribution of APT&C staff. What this simple diagram does not show is the very uneven distribution of women employees within the hierarchy—this is dealt with in more detail in Chapter 9. Here, it may be noted that about 90% of employees in the lowest salary grade are women, while women constitute only some 10% of the principal officer grades. There has, however, been a steady though still small rise in the number of women chief executives, whose numbers approached twenty by mid 1995.

The period from the mid 1980s to mid 1990s has been characterised by large-scale reductions in the numbers of manual employees and teachers. In the manual sector, this has been caused primarily by the impact of compulsory competitive tendering—not just by the loss of work to private contractors, but probably to a greater extent by measures taken by in-house contractor units to enable them to cut costs and so compete successfully with the private sector. The reduction in teacher numbers results partly from a fall in pupil numbers in the late 1980s, together with more recent staffing cuts necessitated by financial restrictions.

Until 1993, the numbers of non-manual staff (excluding teachers) had continued to rise. However, pressure on budgets, together with preparation for white collar CCT and the effect in many authorities of 'delayering' (stripping out intermediate levels in the management hierarchy) led to small but accelerating reductions in white-collar staffing in 1994 and 1995.

❏ Employers' institutions

Types of authorities

Although each local authority is an autonomous employer, there are categories and associations of authorities which have an influence on the staffing characteristics and employment policies of their members. There are, firstly, the five types of authority as established by statute: metropolitan districts, non-metropolitan counties, non-metropolitan districts, London boroughs and the new unitary authorities established as a result of the 1992–95 Local Government Review. Each type has its own range of services and thus its own particular categories of employees. The widely varying size of authorities' workforces between these five types is determined largely by their particular pattern of services. Figure 2.5 shows the way the national workforce is distributed between four of these types of authority. In round figures, and not counting the law and order services, the average number of employees in councils of each type (actual, not full-time equivalents) is:

- non-metropolitan county, 22,000

- metropolitan district, 14,600

- London borough, 8,000

- non-metropolitan district, 770

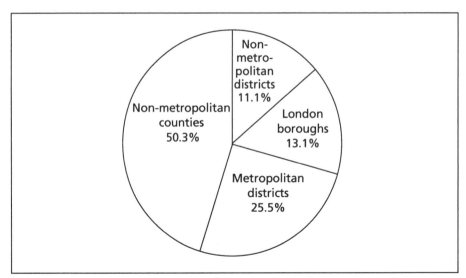

Figure 2.5 Distribution of employees between types of authorities

The main differences in employee categories between the four types of authorities are that the non-metropolitan districts are not responsible for education and consequently employ no teachers; and only the counties employ firefighters. (Figures are not yet available for the new unitaries.)

The associations

There are three national associations of authorities: the Associations of County Councils (ACC), District Councils (ADC) and Metropolitan Authorities (AMA) though discussions were well advanced by the end of 1994 about plans to amalgamate these into a single association. Each acts as a forum for the discussion of issues of particular concern to that type of authority and as a pressure group in relationships with central government. Most of the associations' work is concerned with legal, financial and constitutional matters which are outside the scope of this book, but all three also have personnel sub-committees which examine the implications for their member authorities of employment legislation, consider any manpower issues which are referred to them by their various service committees, and have an input into the evolution of the employers' strategies in the various National Joint Councils which negotiate pay and conditions of service.

The associations operate on much the same lines as local authorities. That is, they are bodies controlled by elected members and conduct their affairs through a committee system. In common with most authorities, their committees reflect the particular services for which each type of authority is responsible. The ACC, for example, has education and social services committees (among others), and major decisions from these service committees are referred to a policy committee, which in turn may require final endorsement from the association's full council. Each association employs a secretariat of professional and administrative staff whose task is to provide the members with appropriate information and advice and administer the committee system.

Elected members serve on the associations' councils and committees through a process of nomination and election by local authorities. Many local authority chief officers are also involved in the work of the associations through being appointed to serve as professional advisers. But while councillors are nominated by their authorities, officer advisers are elected or selected by their various professional societies—an interesting example of the strength and status of the professions in local government. Advisers are consulted by the associations' secretariats on the briefing and advice to be given to the committees, and attend committee meetings (in addition to the associations' own staff) to provide an immediate professional input to the committees' discussions. As professionals, not officer representatives of their employing authorities, they are free to express views which may well not be in accord with the policies of their own councils.

In addition to the three associations, and the employers' sides of the National Joint Councils (dealt with in Chapter 10), there is one other body which has a major involvement in various aspects of employee management, the Local Government Management Board. The Board was established in 1991 as an amalgamation of two organisations:

■ the local Government Training Board (LGTB);

■ the Local Authorities Conditions of Service Advisory Board (LACSAB);

LGMB

Membership of the governing board of the LGMB is by nomination of the ACC, ADC and AMA. The Board oversees the work of a full-time staff and is funded from three main sources—Government grants, subscriptions from local authorities and fees from the sale of some of its services and publications. The LGMB is, in effect, the local government employers' association, a parallel body to organisations in the private sector such as the Engineering Employers Federation. However, the LGMB handles a wider range of functions than many employers' associations. Its activities include:

■ Pay negotiations: national pay bargaining for fifteen different employee groups: information and advice to local authorities on job evaluation, pay and grading, performance management and all aspects of industrial relations.

■ Training: production of a wide range of training material for use by local authorities: the development of NVQs and occupational standards for specific local government jobs; liaison with Training and Enterprise Councils (TECs); promotion of manual worker development.

■ Management development: production of training material for councillors: management development programmes for top managers and women managers.

■ Employment advice: information and advice on UK and EU legislation and case law; advice on pensions.

- Management practice: promoting good practice by identifying and disseminating case study information; advice on management structures and service delivery; information and advice on CCT and local government reorganisation; maintaining a database of management consultants.

- Human resources: promotion of good practice: information and advice on human resource development, appraisal, recruitment, retention and equality issues.

- Research and information: production of pay and other economic statistics: pay and employment surveys; use of census data; monitoring CCT results.

- Examinations: administration of promotion examinations for the police and fire services.

In its training role, the LGMB does not run its own training courses. It produces training material for use by local authorities' own training units and works with other organisations, such as the Management Charter Initiative, in the design of training programmes which are then operated by colleges and other training providers.

The LGMB's industrial relations role includes providing the secretariats for the various National Joint Councils (described in detail in Chapter 10). The Board also provides a forum for representatives of the three local authority associations to discuss and agree broad, strategic policy issues in the field of pay and employment. Two such decisions in recent years are having a major influence on trends in pay and industrial relations:

- That national agreements should increasingly be limited to setting minimum standards for the main conditions of employment, and provide extensive flexibility for authorities to introduce local arrangements to suit their own individual style and circumstances.

- That the traditional differences in the terms and conditions of manual and non-manual employees (blue and white collar) should be phased out—a policy known as harmonisation.

Regional employers' organisations

There are ten regional employers' organisations which originated over fifty years ago with the establishment of Provincial Joint Councils. These Councils consisted of councillors from the local authorities in each region meeting regularly with regional trade union officers to negotiate on pay and other employment matters. Provincial Councils preceded the establishment of National Joint Councils, but as the national system of collective bargaining developed, the scope for regional negotiations slowly diminished.

The employers' sides of the Provincial Councils employed their own full-time secretariats which gradually extended their activities beyond the pay negotiating role and into general advisory and training services. Many were renamed as Regional Employers' Associations or Organisations. When the LGMB was formed, it was agreed that these regional bodies would act as regional LGMB agencies in addition to the services they continued to provide under the direction of their own boards or committees of regionally elected local councillors. These regional employers' organisations have three sources of funding:

- Grants from the LGMB for acting as LGMB regional outlets.

- Subscriptions from the local authorities in their regions.

- Fees paid by their local authorities for specific services, such as employees attending regionally organised training courses, and consultancy work on topics such as local pay systems.

The trend is for an increasing emphasis to be placed on their fee-earning work, so that many of these organisations are now operating to a considerable extent as commercial human resource consultancies.

❑ Employee institutions

Organisations established and run by employees are generally of two kinds:

- professional associations or societies, formed to promote the skills and status of particular specialist groups—accountants, solicitors and the like;

- trade unions, whose main function is to negotiate with the employers about pay and conditions of service, and to provide support and protection to their individual members.

Membership of both types of institution is extensive among local government employees, with many white-collar staff belonging to both. The importance of these institutions in the context of human resource management is that they often have aims and objectives which are not coincident with those of the employer. Japanese management—perhaps the extreme in human resource thinking—works for and expects 100% commitment by the employee to the company. Trade unions, if they exist, are usually company-based. In UK local government, an employee may be in membership of a trade union (say, UNISON), a professional institute which is not a local government body at all (e.g. Institute of Personnel and Development) and a professional local government society which is specific both to a function and to a hierarchical level (e.g. Society of Chief Personnel Officers). Situations will clearly arise in which the interests or values of one or other of the outside organisations will be in conflict with the policy or practices of the employing authority. A high level of commitment to the employer will only be maintained if these potential conflicts of interest, attitude or loyalty are recognised and, if necessary, discussed. An automatic assumption by the employer of a right to expect total dedication may generate the opposite reaction.

Professional institutions

As already noted, many of these bodies have a much wider scope than the world of local government. Many of the white-collar professions operate across all sectors of the economy, public and private. Local government has always relied heavily on the professions for the delivery and management of its services—the reverse of the Civil Service tradition of the general administrator. Accountants manage finance departments, civil engineers manage highways departments, educationalists manage education. Both national and local pay and training systems give positive encouragement to staff to study for relevant professional qualifications. Most authorities, too, give reasonable paid time off to staff who become active in the activities of their various institutes.

Broadly speaking, all these professional bodies have three main functions:

- they claim 'ownership' of a specific body of knowledge which they maintain and up-date; and set and test standards of expertise to which potential members must aspire;
- they produce codes of practice and of professional ethics;
- they promote the status and importance of their professions.

The major refinement or extension of these principles in local government is through those societies which restrict their membership to local government employees and frequently to chief officers. So the chief executive may be a qualified lawyer, but in a local government setting will also join SOLACE, the

Society of Local Authority Chief Executives; while the director of finance will be both an active CIPFA member and a loyal member of the Association of County Treasurers. Note in this latter example that there is a further sub-division—the type of authority, in this case, an association restricted to county chief officers. As noted earlier, professional chief officers' societies are particularly influential through their recognition by the ACC, ADC and AMA as the source of wide-ranging professional advice.

Trade unions

A full discussion of the industrial relations scene is given in Chapter 10. Here, it is important to recognise three general points about trade unions and their influence on human resource management:

■ Trade union membership, while well below the 100% level, is very extensive in local government. While membership has declined over the past ten years, in line with a general trend across the private and public sectors, membership levels are still well above 50% except in some south-eastern authorities. High levels of membership are not necessarily concentrated in the manual or lower white-collar grades. Indeed, one of the sectors which claims 99% membership is at the top, through chief executives' membership of their own trade union, ALACE—the Association of Local Authority Chief Executives.

■ Just as there are many professional societies and a variety of employers' bodies, so too there is a multiplicity of trade unions. Each major occupational group (teachers, manual employees, white-collar workers, etc.) has at least one trade union of its own, often several. Altogether, there are over 25 different unions, each pursuing its own objectives. There has, however, been one major, recent amalgamation of union activity across traditional employee categories. This was the formation in 1993 of the new union, UNISON, by the merger of the white-collar union, NALGO, and the manual union, NUPE. This is dealt with in more detail in Chapter 10.

■ As with professional societies, some unions (the minority) are specific to local government, others have memberships which extend into the private sector and into other public-sector organisations such as the health service.

The implications for management of this pattern of union activity are that while unions are a powerful influence within particular services or employee categories, they rarely act in consort across the whole field. Further, some unions whose main membership and powerbase lies outside local government (such as TGWU, the Transport and General Workers' Union) do not always see things through local government eyes and may have difficulty in understanding or accepting the conventions or limitations which are inherent in a public service. Given their relatively high levels of membership among local government employees, all, however, expect a significant degree of consultation about any plans or problems which might impinge on the jobs or other interests of their members.

Some writers on human resource management in the private sector, particularly in the USA, state or assume that there is little or no role for trade unions. That is not a position which can be maintained in UK local government. While it is right that a greater emphasis should be given than in the past to the development of and communication with the individual employee, managers ignore the collective identity of employees as institutionalised through the trade unions at their peril.

❏ General implications

This chapter has done no more than outline the extremely complex sets of categories and institutions which exist among both employers and employees. Every institution—be it a trade union, employers' association or professional society—has its own particular interests and culture. Every institution has an in-built defensive mechanism; perpetuating its own existence becomes an end in itself—one reason, for example, for the failure of the three main teachers' trade unions to form a single union for an otherwise very homogeneous profession. The existence of all these many different bodies and categories of employees militates against the managerial objective within each local authority of achieving a cohesive, collaborative and committed workforce. Managers consequently need to be aware of these barriers, and then to look for and emphasise common interests rather than reinforce differences. Some examples illustrate this:

- Part-time employees may not see their jobs as so central to their lives as is the case with the full-time, career-minded worker. Their primary concerns may lie in the domestic sphere, or they may have other part-time employment which they think of as more important. This attitude can unwittingly be reinforced by the manager who treats them as peripheral or of less merit than the full-time staff, who fails to explain to them the significance of their work, and who overlooks their training needs. The effective manager provides as much personal recognition, training and general encouragement to part-time as to full-time staff, and builds on the fact that in working only part-time they may be able to retain a higher degree of energy and enthusiasm for the whole of their working time than might be possible for the tiring full-timer.

- Because women are heavily concentrated in the lower levels of the hierarchy, some male managers may assume that they have limited career ambitions. A lack of attention to their real interests and development needs will reinforce this stereotype. The effective manager should be looking to this very large employment sector as an often untapped but potentially very valuable resource of skills and aptitudes.

- A rigid adherence to the prescriptive elements in national agreements may result in an authority's employment conditions failing to promote the qualities needed to meet its service objectives. The effective manager will use every possible discretionary element in these agreements to tailor the conditions of service to meet local needs.

- By highlighting the differences between different trade unions' priorities and sectional interests, it is not difficult to exacerbate divisions between employees. For example, manual employees can be set against their white-collar colleagues by conflicting systems of attendance recording and control. While there may be occasions when this carries a short-term managerial advantage ('divide and rule'), it is no recipe for a harmonious and committed workforce.

- Nationally, the separate identities of the ACC, ADC and AMA have not infrequently weakened the ability of local government as a whole significantly to influence central government policies. Officers who often comment on the desirability of a strong, single voice for local government might ponder on the extent to which they permit the differing pressure and interests of their own professional societies to prejudice the coherence of service or managerial views. By concentrating on the *raison d'être* of local government—public service—a great deal of common ground can be established between the professions, and between various categories of employees, and the great benefits of a high level of professional expertise can be harnessed to the achievement of vital service objectives.

QUESTIONS ABOUT YOUR OWN AUTHORITY

- Is the composition of the workforce (by category, occupation, gender, age, service, etc.) regularly monitored?

- Do members and officers ensure that advice and comment to national bodies such as LGMB is co-ordinated and consistent with the authority's overall policies?

- Is effective use made of information and advisory services provided by regional and national bodies?

- Are policies or objectives sometimes unduly biased by the interests of external institutions?

- Is public service seen as the shared objective of otherwise differing interests?

3

People and organisations

KEY POINTS

- No jobs are self-contained—all interact.

- Organisation structures divide work vertically into hierarchical levels, and horizontally into functions.

- There is a trend towards flatter, simpler, more flexible structures.

- Over-complex work systems lead to waste and conflict.

- A useful guideline is: centralisation of policy, decentralisation of practice.

- An authority's culture—its values and style—needs to be consistent with its perceived priorities and objectives. Culture has to be managed.

- Managers have a crucial role in imparting to the workforce a vision of the authority's character and purpose.

Whether directly, or by commissioning from external providers, one of the primary functions of a local authority is the provision of a wide range of public services. These are, in effect, the authority's output. To achieve this output, there has to be an input of resources (money, people, equipment), and these resources have to be activated. The nature of this output is determined by what the authority perceives as the external needs, requirements, pressures or opportunities. The internal activation of resources can be thought of, quite simply, as 'work'. Figure 3.1 illustrates this concept.

Managers often think of work in terms of employees doing jobs, and of work design in terms of individual job descriptions. But the management of work is much more complex than the management of employees as individuals. Except in a one-person business, individual jobs are never self-contained. Every job has working links with others. These links may be vertical—up to senior management, down to subordinates—or horizontal, with sideways contacts with other jobs from which information is obtained, or to and from

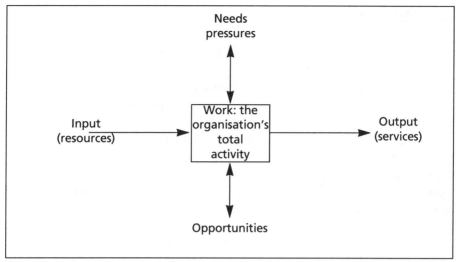

Figure 3.1 The organisation of work

which partially completed sequences of work are passed. All the jobs, with all their linkages, form 'the organisation', and its design has a major influence on its effectiveness in achieving the authority's desired output or service objectives. Inadequate or inappropriate organisational structures or systems can generate problems which the manager may perceive initially as 'human'.

For example, the stores' manager in one authority had a reputation for being awkward and unhelpful when the social services department needed urgent deliveries of bed linen to cope with unexpected emergency admissions to children's homes. It was thought that a change of person in this post would lead to better working relationships. An organisation and systems study suggested otherwise. First, it was shown that the place of the stores' manager in the supplies department's hierarchy inhibited his ability to do other than stick to standard routines. Secondly, it became clear that, for most urgent needs, the social services department should hold their own emergency stock of bed linen.

Similarly, friction between two section or department heads can not unusually be shown to stem from their formally defined responsibilities being in conflict. Understanding how organisations function is consequently of considerable importance to managers. Three main factors are involved:

■ structures;

■ systems or procedures;

■ organisational culture.

❏ Structures

Most managers are familiar with traditional organisation charts—the 'family tree'. It is worth looking behind these charts to examine the basis on which they can be built up. Figure 3.1 showed a single box, labelled 'Work: the organisation's total activity'. In a one-person business, that box would also represent the one person's job. In larger organisations, more people are needed and the total work has therefore to be divided up into job-sized pieces. How is this done? As Figure 3.2 shows, work is divided into levels— the job hierarchy—with chief officers and the chief executive at the top, through senior, middle and junior management to supervision and the shop or office floor.

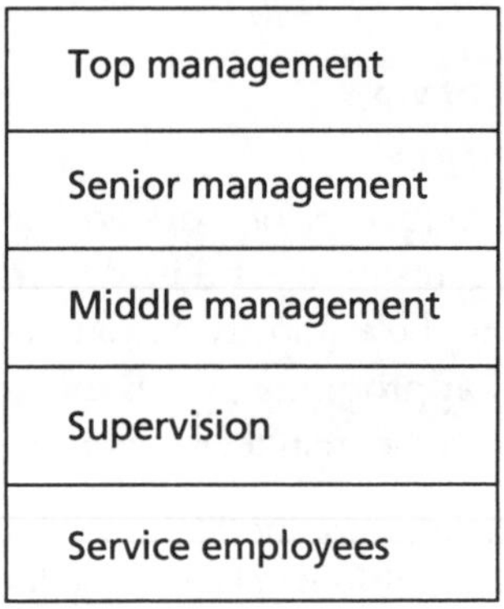

Top management
Senior management
Middle management
Supervision
Service employees

Figure 3.2 Hierarchical division of organisation's total activity

The hierarchical division goes only halfway towards a full sub-division of work. Work also has to be divided into parallel groupings, and there is a variety of options as to how this might be done. The main alternatives are:

■ by service—the traditional division of a local authority into departments: housing, planning and so on;

■ by function—to some extent a variation on the service theme, with sub-divisions for, say, finance, personnel, office administration, legal and the like;

■ by geographical area—such as the area office structure frequently used in education and social services; or the divisional structure common in highways departments;

- by user group—used, again, in education and social services to establish separate divisions for, say, children's and adults' services;

- by occupation or profession—such as a maintenance unit which is sub-divided by building trades (painters, carpenters, etc.); or a property management department which has separate sections for architects, quantity surveyors and valuers.

As a result of compulsory competitive tendering, many functional and service divisions are having to be further subdivided into client and contractor units. The client unit is concerned with identifying the authority's needs, converting these into formal specifications, and then—through a tendering process—purchasing what is required from in-house or external sources. The contractor unit (often termed a business unit) is the in-house provider, bidding for work in competition with commercial contractors and consultants. Some authorities, by adopting the principles of the internal market, have applied this client/contractor (or purchaser/provider) model more widely than just for the services subject to CCT. They have established client and contractor units throughout all or most of their functions, though the primary emphasis has been to use this model for support services such as finance, personnel, IT and legal services.

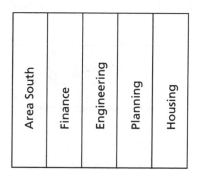

Figure 3.3 Forms of parallel subdivision—by service, function, geographical area

Figure 3.3 shows this parallel form of sub-division while Figure 3.4 illustrates how the combination of the hierarchical and parallel sub-divisions results in the total work of the organisation being chopped up into pieces, each of which constitutes one person's work—a job.

Structural options

It can be seen from this simple analysis that many options exist in the design of organisational structures. How many levels should there be in the hierarchy? What type of parallel division should predominate? In discussing structural design, it is essential to accept that there is no one best pattern for all local authorities. There is an interaction between structure, system and culture. Structural design cannot be isolated from the design of work procedures and systems and, to be effective, structure and system must be wholly compatible with, and reinforce, the individual authority's values, style and service priorities. This book cannot, therefore, recommend any particular structure for general application. It can, though, suggest factors which need to be considered.

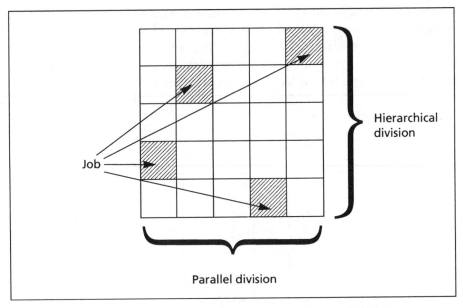

Figure 3.4 Hierarchical and parallel divisions combined to produce jobs

Hierarchical levels

Local authorities have tended to have tall, multi-level hierarchies. To quote Elliott Jaques in his *General theory of bureacracy* (Heineman, 1976): 'It is an almost universal disease of bureaucratic systems that they have too many levels.' There are still relatively small authorities with as many as nine different levels—chief executive, chief officer, deputy chief officer, assistant chief officer, divisional manager, assistant divisional manager, section manager, section supervisor, service workers.

Simple arithmetic will show that if each manager and supervisor in a nine-level hierarchy has just five subordinates, the total number employed will be nearly half a million! Looked at a different way, if every manager and supervisor has eight subordinates, then only four levels are needed for a total workforce of around 1,300—the size of many district councils.

There is obviously more than simple arithmetic involved in actual structural design, and reducing the number of levels simply to keep rigidly to a formula would be most unwise. The pros and cons of tall and flat hierarchies are worth examining:

- In tall structures, managers can exercise close control over subordinate functions.

- Tall structures, which are coincident with small control spans, may also free managers from any heavy time involvement with dealing with subordinates' problems.

- Tall structures offer more promotion opportunities.

- In tall structures, however, top management can become remote or isolated from actual service delivery.

- Flat structures facilitate more rapid decision-making.

- Flat structures reduce the volume of internal administration or communication which is needed between levels.

- Tall structures necessitate narrow salary bands; in flat structures, more salary progression can be built into individual job grades.

There has been a marked trend towards flatter structures and fewer levels can be seen in many authorities which have redesigned their structures. In industry this trend has become so marked that it has acquired its own jargon description—'de-layering'. The process is aided by the application of information technology.

For example, a large county council used to operate its social services on a three-tier system—HQ, three geographical divisions, and six or seven area offices in each division. In a delayering exercise, the divisional tier was removed entirely. It was stated that this simplification of structure was achievable only by the computer linkage of each area to HQ to facilitate instant communication (by electronic mail) and to make HQ data on client records and service expenditure immediately available to the area staff.

A checklist of factors which need to be considered in any exercise of organisational design is:

- The degree to which the managed jobs are similar in content. The more similarity, the more can be managed.

- The physical contiguity of subordinate staff. The fewer separate locations, the more can be managed.

- The complexity of the managed functions. The more complex, the fewer can be managed.

- The intensity of supervision required. The more intensive the supervision, the fewer the direct subordinates.

- The extent of co-ordination necessary with other managers' functions. If the manager has to spend much time in 'sideways' co-ordination, he or she has less time for the supervisory role.

- The extent of planning and programming required. Again, if these activities occupy much of the manager's time, less time will be available for supervision.

- The availability of assistance with the management of the subordinate functions from other managers or specialists. Thus, a finance specialist might relieve the manager of tasks which would otherwise erode the supervisory role.

Parallel divisions

Conventionally, the primary division of local authorities' activities is by service—housing, planning, education and so on. These form the first sub-division into departments below the chief executive. Within departments, there can be a variety of sub-divisions, though the two most common are by function (finance, office services, personnel, etc.) and geography (area offices). Within any one department, all conceivable types of sub-division may be used.

For example, in one social services department, the service side is first sub-divided into two client group divisions—children's and adults' services. The whole service is then split geographically into six areas. Within each area office there is a functional split into finance and staffing. At HQ, there is a similar functional division with finance and personnel units, but additionally there are several groups which constitute occupational division such as occupational therapists and advisers for services to the visually impaired.

Senior management has to undertake a good deal of internal co-ordination and communication to keep all these differently structured pieces of the whole service synchronised.

What is often lacking in the process of organisational design is any strong, single theme or objective to provide coherence. Conventionally, two powerful influences are at work, though neither may be articulated. First, there is the tendency for professions to maintain and enhance their own separate identity and status. An architect's department had been structured by occupation with separate sections of design architects, quantity surveyors, structural engineers, building engineers, heating and ventilation engineers and so on. The chief officer wished to achieve a much more collaborative approach, and restructured the department into four multi-disciplinary geographical divisions. There was an initial outcry from each of the major professional groups that this plan reduced their professional identity and status. There was also reaction from the quantity surveyors and engineers to the selection of four architects to head the four new multi-functional divisions. This was seen as the ranking of one profession above the others—though the appointments were seen by the authority as managerial, not professional.

The second influence is a tendency to structure an authority to suit its internal administrative convenience, rather than that of the community. Given the preference for functional or occupational patterns, the result from the viewpoint of the individual citizen is that he or she has to relate to many different parts of the authority. Thus, one authority dealt with the award of student grants in two departments. Education assessed grant applications against award criteria; the finance department processed the actual payments. Following public complaints, a study showed that 40% of enquiries from students about the progress of their grant applications needed attention by both departments. Enquirers, however, were given half the answer by one department and then told to make separate approaches to the second department—which was in a different location. Administratively, each department found it convenient to deal only with its own part of the process. The two sections were later amalgamated.

Over the past decade, a single, dominating theme has emerged which is causing fundamental re-assessments by many authorities of the effects of their structures and systems on the quality of their services. The theme is 'public service orientation', the recognition that effective, helpful, efficient service to the public is the primary aim and test of every service. It is for this reason that some authorities have begun to develop the concept of the 'one-stop office'—conveniently located contact points where the public can hopefully get answers on any local authority topic. This may, of course, leave the conventional departmental structure unchanged, with the contact office acting as an intermediary between the citizen and a whole range of separate services. More fundamental is the area management concept in which multi-service operations are set up on a geographical basis. In effect, each operates as a mini authority and, in the most highly developed systems, is matched by all-purpose area committees.

If public service is the unifying factor in terms of an authority's external purpose, simplicity of structure and system is a good internal guide. A major international management consultant, W. J. Reddin, has suggested that the best indicator of a need for structural change is a lack of clarity as to how the structure works. In any redesign, Reddin looks for 'simplicity about who is responsible for what and where decisions are made' (*The best of Bill Reddin* IPM, 1982).

❏ Systems

This leads on to the systems side of the interaction between structure and system. Complex structures generate complex systems as each level or parallel function is drawn into a decision-making or service-delivery process. Equally, complex procedures can generate complex structures as separate jobs or sections evolve to handle different elements in a process. Complexity leads to narrowly defined jobs, simplicity leads to job enlargement.

It is helpful to have a picture of what constitutes most systems or procedures. Figure 3.5 shows, in simplified form, a group of jobs defined by hierarchy and parallel function. The arrowed lines represent the passage of a process—say, a request from a pensioner for a home-help—through the organisation. The request may be received initially by a telephone call to a clerk at an area office. She refers it to a fieldwork supervisor, who passes it to a social worker to investigate. The social worker reports back with a recommendation which is passed to the appropriate home-help organiser. Further parts of the whole process involve administrative staff in the social services and finance departments setting up and recording charges, while from the pensioner's viewpoint, the final output is the arrival of a home-help.

It is the whole network of such chains of activity which bind the individual jobs in the structure into a productive whole. The value of simplicity is that the fewer linkages or separate stages in a process, the quicker decisions can be made and output achieved, and the less risk there is of misunderstandings or delays occurring in the passage of the process between separate jobs. Every arrowed line in Figure 3.5 carries this risk.

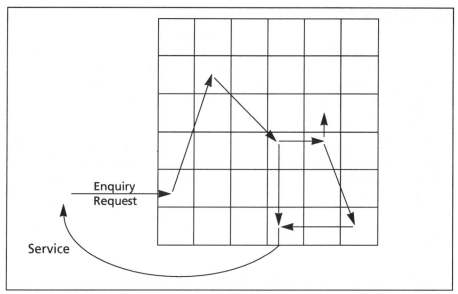

Figure 3.5 Passage of a procedure between jobs, and to and from original external initiating point

It is a feature of most organisations, though particularly the less effective, that major differences develop between the formally prescribed systems and those by which staff actually get their jobs done. Within limits, this may be of benefit. A too-lengthy chain of command may regularly be by-passed in order to reduce delays. Managers may use their good sense and initiative to make sensible, informal adjustments, and operational staff will often discover useful short-cuts. But two dangers remain:

■ The informal by-passing or simplification of formal systems will leave some jobs, levels or functions in formal existence long past the point at which they should have been disbanded. A redundant level in the hierarchy is an extremely expensive luxury.

■ Informal systems may develop to a point at which they are in direct conflict with authority policy. Managerial reluctance fully to implement an equal opportunity policy, for example, may result in the formal system of monitoring applicants falling into desuetude—to the detriment of the policy.

Centralisation, decentralisation and devolution

Discussions about the design of structures and systems often develop into over-simplified arguments for or against decentralisation. Because each authority needs to determine its own style of operation, there can be no single answer to a question as to whether or not decentralisation is a good thing. In any event, this question is misleading. Some aspects of an authority's function may require a concentration of attention at the centre (usually meaning at the top of the management hierarchy and by elected members), others may be best dealt with on a highly decentralised basis in the field. Centralisation and decentralisation are not mutually exclusive.

While a standard solution is inappropriate, there is a general trend of thinking which is being reflected in many authorities' redesigns of organisation. In the private sector, this has been described (in *In Search of Excellence*, Peters and Waterman, Harper and Row, 1982) as 'simultaneous loose–tight properties'. What this means, in the words of one local authority which has taken a conscious decision to restructure on this principle, is 'centralisation of policy, decentralisation of practice'.

Within the systems, decision-making will be pushed as far down the line as possible to achieve speed and responsiveness. The more clearly policies and the parameters of decision-making are centrally articulated and pursued, the more freedom to act can be delegated, because the aims and boundaries of action are defined. It is ambiguity and the lack of policy direction from the centre which often leads to an unintended centralisation of practice, as the lower levels of staff keep pushing issues up the line for guidance or approval. How this approach can be developed in practice can be shown by an example. One large authority had a conventionally centralised finance department. Service departments handled very few financial processes. All budgetary control information was issued from the centre. It was a common complaint of the finance department that service departments were not sufficiently cost-conscious, and of service departments that finance burdened them with obsessively detailed requirements for reporting even the most miniscule items of expenditure—and provided incomprehensible budget data. In a major review of structure and systems, the authority established finance sections in each major department, responsible to service chief officers, though staffed by accountants transferred from central finance. Systems were redesigned to provide the control information which service departments needed and which they themselves now had the responsibility and resource to produce. The central role was changed from large-scale processing of routine operations to the strategic management and oversight of the financial resource, and to the maintenance of financial standards.

Particularly for support functions such as finance and personnel, it is helpful to distinguish between decentralisation and devolution. Decentralisation involves the slimming of large, central support service departments, with operational departments and Direct Service Organisations (DSOs) then having their own accountants and personnel staff. Devolution involves line managers undertaking tasks (such as trade union negotiation or budget planning) which have previously been handled by specialists.

Devolution raises important and sometimes difficult issues in the personnel field. Legally, a local authority is a single employer and much employment legislation and case law expects an employer to display consistency across all divisions or departments in matters such as disciplinary standards, the evaluation of jobs for pay purposes, and the provision of alternative employment to avoid redundancies. If managers in individual departments or units have been given devolved powers to make their own decisions about such matters, the question arises as to how any form of corporate consistency is to be maintained. Several highly devolved authorities have addressed this issue by defining broad, key principles or standards for the management of people, while leaving managers free to apply these principles in whatever way is appropriate to their particular services. One county council explained this approach by stating that managers were now free to manage their own staff—provided they did so to an acceptable standard. This standard (or set of standards) was described in a document entitled 'Specification for Devolved Human Resource Management'. To take one example from this document, it stated as a matter of corporate principle that all staff should have at least an annual appraisal interview and this must should cover both work-based objectives and individual training needs. Managers were free, however, to evolve their own detailed appraisal systems—provided each system complied with the corporate principles.

❑ Organisational culture

The concept of organisational culture has become a significant theme in academic and practical management thinking. However, it lacks a generally agreed definition and, as a result, is a term used in somewhat different ways by different theorists or practitioners. Some suggest a very simple definition such as Peters' (*In Search of Excellence*) 'the way we do things around here'. Others find this too imprecise to be of much help and extend the definition to include strategies, values and beliefs.

For the purpose of this book, culture is used as a term derived from anthropology. When anthropologists study and describe the culture of a tribe, they examine the tribe's environment, its primary economic or survival activity (e.g. farming, cattle herding, hunting), its social structure, its customs, values and beliefs. The resultant whole 'way of life' is, in effect, the tribal culture.

This is a useful analogy because it emphasises how important it is for survival for the economic function to be in harmony with the environment, for the social structure to be appropriate to the main function, for customs to reinforce successful patterns of conduct and activity, and all to be held together by a common bond of belief in those qualities which are essential to survival and success. Thus the Masai in Kenya are, or were, a successful cattle-herding tribe because cattle-herding is natural to the grassy plains of the Serengeti, their social structure is decentralised into the small, largely autonomous groups which are necessary for a peripatetic function, their customs create a necessary degree of common identity to prevent conflict between otherwise potentially conflicting autonomous groups, and the qualities they value—physical prowess and individual bravery—are of great importance in protecting their herds from attack by predators. This is, of course, a highly condensed and simplified description, but it illustrates some critically important issues.

Very much the same kind of analysis can be applied to a local authority. What is the social, economic and legal environment within which it operates? Are its activities in harmony or in conflict with these external constraints and opportunities? Does its organisational structure aid or inhibit the effective operation of its functions? Do its systems and procedures fit the shape of its structure? What qualities does it consider important, and are these congruent with the nature of its functions, and with the shape or style of its structure and systems. What effect is the separation of client and contractor functions for CCT having on the quality and characteristics of internal relationships and attitudes?

There is, though, one major difference between the tribe and the authority. Tribal culture evolves through a very long-term and unconscious evolutionary process. Few such cultures incorporate rapid adaptability to major environmental or economic change. Culture as a management concept has been developed on the basis that an organisation can consciously determine its own desired style and cultural characteristics, and achieve cultural change by a planned management process.

There is very much more to a programme of cultural change than producing a new council logo, adopting a slogan such as 'Exshire: Your Caring Council', and sending reception staff to a charm school. Indeed, superficial action of this kind will probably make matters worse. From the public's viewpoint, all that may change is that the authority's inefficiency becomes courteous, while staff still working to unnecessarily complex or rigid systems will become very cynical about what they will see as no more than a public relations exercise. Some authorities, though, have embarked on comprehensive and fundamental programmes of cultural change. They have found it valuable to set such programmes within a framework of stated values – the key qualities against which the authority judges its reputation and performance.

One district council in 1993 set itself the objective of changing from a static to an adaptable culture, and began by defining its core values as:

- support for the democratic process;

- responsiveness to the needs of the community and service users;

- fairness and openness;

- partnership working with other organisations;

- prudence in the management of the council's assets.

The widespread changes to structures and systems which were then introduced were designed to promote these values, and the implications for the nature of jobs, staff training, employee communications, pay systems and management style were also addressed. The whole process was managed as a co-ordinated programme, with the realisation that a change to any one element had an effect on all or most of the others.

The whole process of reviewing and changing structures and systems has been termed organisational development, and it is useful to consider this as the collective or institutional equivalent of management development. Management development is concerned with ensuring that managers as individuals understand the needs of their jobs and acquire the attitudes, knowledge and skills to achieve optimum individual performance. Organisational development is concerned with ensuring that the whole authority knows what it is doing and where it is going, and develops the characteristics needed to achieve these aims.

Human resource implications

It may be thought that many of the concepts dealt with in this chapter are fairly far removed from the day-to-day management of staff: that organisational issues are not really part of human resource management.

It needs to be recognised, however, that structures and systems do not exist separately from the people who make them work. They are no more than the mechanisms which enable people to work together effectively. Further, how well an authority's human resource 'drives' this mechanism is vitally dependent on the motivation, commitment, understanding and skills of employees at all levels.

It is because of this that culture—in the sense of style and values—is so important, and the role of managers so crucial. The word vision has been used—an essentially human attribute. Impersonal structures and systems cannot have vision—that is something which only people can bring. To quote from a report produced by the Audit Commission:

> *Vision means having an understanding of where your authority should be going, how it should be run and the philosophies which should underly its actions . . .*
>
> *Although vision may be expressed through strategic planning and policy making processes, its greatest influence is likely to come through the development of a shared culture. This often involves some unifying concepts that bring people together . . .*
>
> *Where all the individuals within an organisation accept similar beliefs and values about its purpose and their work, then vision can be expressed at all levels and in a multiplicity of activities . . .*
>
> *For vision to become important and influential, there are two prerequisites. First there must be a strong and almost inspired leadership . . .*
>
> *Second there must be a pattern of systems and structures which reinforces what is to be achieved, rather than militates against it . . .*

This chapter has concentrated on structures and systems. As the quotation indicates, this must be linked to staff motivation and leadership—a topic dealt with in more detail in Chapter 6.

QUESTIONS ABOUT YOUR AUTHORITY

- How many levels are there in the management hierarchy? Could the number be reduced?

- How is the organisation structured functionally? Could the structure be simplified?

- Are work systems subject to review? Are any procedures or parts of procedures superfluous?

- Are decisions taken as close as possible to where they take effect?

- Does the authority's culture reinforce the skills and attitudes necessary for the achievement of the authority's aims?

- Do managers have, and impart to the workforce, a clear vision of the authority's purpose and priorities?

4

Recruitment and selection

KEY POINTS

- Staff selection merits as much care as the choice of capital equipment.

- Effective selection requires:
  —analysis and definition of the job (job description);
  —choice of appropriate salary and conditions;
  —definition of the qualities required (person specification);
  —targeting of recruitment;
  —use of an appropriate array of selection methods.

- Selection should not rely solely on interviews—other methods include written and group tasks, and ability and personality tests.

The first chapter of this book emphasised the extent to which the effective delivery of local government services was dependent on the ability and attitudes of local authorities' staff. Two employees may have the same qualifications and experience and be equally skilful in terms of professional or technical expertise. But while one is interested, enthusiastic and committed, the other is bored or disgruntled. The degree of difference between them in terms of work performance will not be marginal—it will probably vary by a massive factor.

No manager would quarrel with the view that recruiting and selecting staff is therefore of vital importance. Yet in practice, the amount of attention paid to staff selection contrasts strangely with the effort normally put into the choice of equipment or software.

In the early 1990s, a council decided it needed a new management information system. A four-person project team was charged with the task of assessing alternative software. The team had detailed discussions with numerous potential suppliers and visited organisations using the systems under review. After four months' study, the team produced a report and recommendations which was discussed at length by the top management team, before a final proposal was submitted to the policy and resources committee. The cost of the review in terms of staff time and travel was about £35,000. The annual licensing and support costs of the selected software was approximately £40,000.

Soon after this review, the chief executive was due to retire. An advertisement for a replacement, at a salary of £50,000 was placed in the local government press. The retiring chief executive and the council leader spent a day reading the resultant applications and selecting five candidates for interview. Each had an hour's informal discussion with the retiring chief executive, and a forty-five minute interview by a panel of elected members. When the interviews had been completed, the panel ranked the candidates in order of preference. There was general agreement about the first choice, but some differences of view about the others. However, these differences were not discussed in any detail.

The appointment was offered to the panel's preferred candidate, who initially accepted the offer. However, two weeks before he was due to take up the appointment he withdrew. The council leader consulted his colleagues by telephone and decided to offer the job to the candidate who had been the panel's second choice—who accepted. Within six months it had become evident that the appointment was a mistake, though no action was taken for a further eighteen months, during which staff morale in the authority was badly affected. A termination package costing £75,000 was eventually negotiated.

The contrast—in terms of time, cost and care—between the selection of the software package and the choice of a chief executive is very obvious, despite the potential direct and indirect costs of making a bad decision for a top management appointment.

The limited effort sometimes put into staff selection is not, however, just a matter of inadequate care. There are real problems involved, and one major difference between the assessment of equipment and candidates for employment.

The main practical problem is that recruitment goes on all the time as staff leave or retire and as new jobs are established. An authority employing 2,500 staff may have to recruit about 200 new employees each year to replace leavers. If an average of six candidates are to be assessed for each vacancy, this implies 1,200 to be seen each year, or over 20 each week. Busy managers do not have the time to operate very lengthy selection procedures for this volume of recruitment.

The problem is compounded by the main difference between the selection of employees and equipment. For the latter it is normally possible to produce very specific, often quantified, criteria which are capable of statistical measurement or similarly objective assessment. This is not the case with employee selection. It may be possible to specify some requirements of fact (e.g. the possession of a particular qualification) but success or failure in appointments is very heavily influenced by the more intangible qualities of interest, imagination, commitment and personality.

The fact that it is more difficult to select staff than equipment is no reason, though, for treating the task more casually—rather the reverse. It is possible to improve the selection success rate by following a logical and planned process. This needs to consider:

- the nature of the work—the job and its purpose;

- the appropriate conditions—pay, hours, etc;

- the qualities required—the person specification;

- the target sector for recruitment;

- the appropriate selection methods.

❏ Defining the job

It is impossible to select effectively without a clear picture of the work to be done, and how the various elements of this work are structured to form a job. It is equally important for applicants that they should know what the job involves. A written job description serves both purposes: it provides the basis for the selection process and enables applicants to decide whether or not the job is of real interest.

To be of most use, job descriptions need to be biased towards defining the range of duties—what actually has to be done—rather than concentrating on responsibilities. To say, for example, that a departmental finance officer is 'responsible for budgetary control information' does not help a great deal with specifying the knowledge and skills required. The statement is too general, too imprecise. Many authorities have adopted a style of job description in which one general statement about the overall purpose of the job is followed by a list of key activities or duties. Here is an example of this type, taken from a council's property management department.

Job title: Building engineer
Grade: SO1/2
Responsible to: Area Property Manager
Responsible for: Team of 5–8 building technicians
Purpose of job:

To assess the repair and maintenance requirements of all council buildings within a designated area, and manage the letting and supervision of repair and maintenance contracts.

Main Job Duties:

1. Plan and effect a schedule of building inspections.
2. Produce for management approval, schedules of repair and maintenance work.
3. Liaise with contracts section on production of tender specifications.
4. Monitor contractors' performance and ensure compliance with contract requirements.
5. Authorise variations within designated limits.
6. Manage, train and develop team of technicians.
7. Any other relevant duties allocated by area manager.

Note the emphasis in this example on the verbs—the 'doing' words—plan, produce, liaise, monitor, authorise, manage, etc. It is from these that a picture can be built up of the qualities needed to do the job well. To plan and produce schedules implies a systematic, analytical ability. To liaise, monitor and authorise indicates a need for negotiating or inter-personal skills.

Note, too, in this example that the list of duties is set out briefly and without any attempt to be wholly comprehensive. There is sometimes a tendency to set down every conceivable activity on the mistaken basis that if something is not in the job description it cannot be required to be done. This idea originates with the bad practice of incorporating job descriptions into contracts of employment, something which is neither legally necessary nor managerially desirable. Over-lengthy job descriptions can impose rigidity on the way work is carried out without adding to the necessary understanding of the essential characteristics needed for job success.

When a vacancy occurs, recruitment is sometimes based on the original job description. It is always as well to check this—and, indeed, to start by asking whether the job is needed at all. Could the duties be allocated to other posts? Have the duties or work relationships changed since the last person was appointed? Does the vacancy provide an opportunity for some redesign of structure or system? Are there different emphases in the work? Only when questions of this type have been resolved should the job description be finalised.

❏ Job conditions

When producing or revising the definition of a job, its general conditions also need review. Is the wage or grade still appropriate? Does it still need to be a full-time job? Might it be suitable for job-sharing? Does it have to be done on a standard five-day, 9–5 basis? Is a car required?

As with the design of the job itself, the occurrence of a vacancy, or the creation of a new post, provides an opportunity for some very fundamental questions to be asked which can have a major influence on recruitment. For example, one authority was experiencing great difficulty in recruiting accountants. It was realised that all such work had previously been structured into conventional full-time jobs and that this might be limiting the field of applicants. Yet there were many elements of the work which did not have to be undertaken on a strict 9–5, Monday to Friday basis, 52 weeks a year. It was therefore decided to advertise accountancy vacancies in many other patterns of working time—part-time, evenings, school term-time only. This resulted in a number of appointments being made, mainly of women who for domestic reasons were unable to take up 'normal' full-time jobs.

Another consideration is the type or duration of the employment contract. A significant trend in recent years has been the use of fixed-term contracts for senior managers—usually for between three and five years. There have been two main reasons for this development. First, the expiry of a fixed-term contract gives the authority an opportunity to make a change of appointment without having to become involved in any form of enforced termination. This may be of particular advantage when there has been a change of political control or when an authority wants to achieve a major change of style. Secondly, for the manager concerned, a fixed-term contract may offer greater job security for its duration than a conventional open-ended contract. It may also offer a somewhat higher salary to compensate for the risk of its not being renewed on its expiry.

Person specifications

Once the job and its conditions have been defined, the next step is to consider and specify the qualities and characteristics to be looked for in applicants. Too often, this essential step is either overlooked or it is assumed that what is being looked for in applicants are the characteristics of the last job-holder—provided he or she was reasonably satisfactory.

Just as with the design of the job itself, recruitment provides an opportunity to take stock and ask whether experience or changing circumstances indicate a need for a change. Perhaps the job has always been filled previously by young people, who stay a few years and then move up to bigger appointments. Is this the only or best way for the work to be done? Perhaps someone over 50 might bring useful experience and maturity to the section. It may have been customary to limit selection to graduates. Is this really necessary?

The person specification needs to be thought through and defined, taking into account only those factors which are clearly necessary if the job is to be done satisfactorily.

These factors will obviously vary from job to job, but some authorities find it helpful to use a checklist of standard headings. An example from a metropolitan district is given below:

1. Job knowledge—technical, specialist or professional.
2. Job skills—manual, intellectual, creative, social.
3. Personality factors—e.g. resilience, sociability, conformity or innovativeness, etc.
4. Circumstances—e.g. ability to travel, work unsocial hours, etc.

A more conventional list will probably include educational standards, qualifications, experience, and technical or professional skill, as well as some indication of social skills or key personality traits.

There are two particular points to guard against:

- There is a marked tendency to over-specify the requirements for such factors as educational standards and length of work experience, when the emphasis should be on the minimum satisfactory level. Over-qualified staff soon become frustrated in jobs which are too small for them: the best appointees are often those whose new jobs represent a greater challenge and are more stretching than their previous work.

- A related fault is to specify too narrowly. At its worst, this can be seen in the occasional prescription that there is a preferred age limit of, say, 28 to 35. It occurs, too, in placing limitations on qualifications—such as an insistence that all accountants, regardless of their differing jobs, have to hold CIPFA membership. Many restricted specifications are also unwittingly discriminatory against women or ethnic minorities. For example, restricting trainee entry to certain permutations of age and qualification may well make such posts inaccessible for women returning to work after a domestic career break. Similarly, criteria about standards of written English may be quite unnecessary for the actual work, but will prevent the recruitment of many Asian women.

❑ Recruitment targeting

The specification leads on to consideration of the sources from which applicants should be sought; and this in turn influences the nature of the recruitment campaign and the choice of advertising or recruitment media.

As with other aspects of the whole process, there is a tendency to repeat past practice. It may have become a habit, for example, to rely entirely on word-of-mouth recruitment for refuse collectors or to use just two local government publications to advertise all APT&C vacancies. Even the wording of advertisements may have become standardised. What such practices are doing is slowly to narrow the field of potential employees and to reinforce the existing characteristics of the workforce. Word-of-mouth recruitment is a particularly strong influence of this kind and is strongly condemned by all the agencies working in the field of equal opportunities. One London borough, with a large black population, had relied for years on word-of-mouth recommendations from the existing workforce in its recruitment of building-craft apprentices. All were white, at a time of massive unemployment among black school-leavers. The recruitment process was changed to open advertising and a systematic and objective selection procedure. Within three years the number of black apprentices reflected the population characteristics of the borough, and the quality of recruits had risen.

For some jobs, it has also become customary to rely entirely on unsolicited applications. A number of fire services maintain waiting lists of such applicants. This may not be so obviously undesirable as word-of-mouth recruitment, but it is not sound practice. It assumes that the public at large understand the nature of the work and know the kind of applicant the authority prefers—and such assumptions may be incorrect. The very small number of black people and women applying for jobs of this kind probably indicates that the local community sees the authority as preferring white men.

The emphasis on equal opportunity issues throughout this chapter is important and stems directly from the human resource philosophy. It is an essential part of this thinking that the effective and healthy organisation needs to draw on the widest possible range of human talent. Local government faces massive problems and challenges from social, economic and political change. It will meet these challenges most effectively if its workforce reflects the make-up of the community, and includes a much wider range of skills, understanding and attitude than can be provided by traditionally narrow sources of recruitment and selection.

There is thus a need to consider many more sources of recruitment than conventional advertising in the local and specialist press; and advertisements need to be written to match the media used. For example, authorities who complain that they receive too few applications from the private sector may be using the same wording in the national as local government press. Salary statements such as 'PO 42–46 (under review)' not only mean nothing outside the local government world, they probably give a directly adverse impression. One authority uses the following checklist of recruitment sources:

- Advertisements: Local government journals
  Local press
  National daily or Sunday press
  Trade and special-interest journals
  Journals of professional bodies
  Ethnic-minority press
  Community news-sheets
  University, college or school magazines
  Local radio and television;

- Job Centres;

- The Careers Service;

- School, college and university careers services;

- Private-sector employment agencies;

- Management consultants;

- Executive search consultants.

❏ Selection methods

The ultimate test of the whole recruitment and selection process is, of course, whether the final choice of candidate proves successful. Mention selection and most managers immediately think of interviewing as the main or often sole method of making this crucial decision. Interviews are, and always will be, the most important single selection technique, but they are by no means the only method. Relying solely on interviews means placing too much reliance on a single technique which no experienced interviewer would ever claim as infallible.

It is worth listing a much wider range of methods:

- single, rather than panel, interviews;
- CV analysis;
- reference enquiries;
- written tasks;
- group tasks;
- tests of many kinds.

Interviews

Before examining other methods, it is important that managers do all they can to achieve the highest possible standard of interviewing. This is best done by attending a specific training course which provides interview practice under coaching. Some authorities consider this so important that they do not allow any manager or elected member to take part in selection interviewing unless they have satisfactorily completed such a course. The subject cannot be given comprehensive consideration here, but some key principles are:

- A balance of views is best obtained by having more than one interviewer—though this does not necessarily imply a panel. The best results may be achieved by two or three interviewers conducting single interviews in sequence, having agreed in advance that each concentrates on a particular aspect.

- The practical arrangements must be efficient: with courteous, helpful reception, adequate waiting facilities, and an explanation to the candidates about the nature of the selection process.

- Within an interview, the interviewer should do as little talking as possible. Interviews are not debates or opportunities for managers to demonstrate their knowledge or wit. The interviewer's task is to get the candidate talking and to listen.

- Open-ended questions should be asked—those which cannot be answered by 'yes' or 'no'. Open-ended questions start: 'Tell us about ...' 'What do you think of ...' 'Say a little more about ...'

- Generalised answers should be probed. Thus a candidate for a library appointment may be asked for an example of a major initiative. He or she may reply: 'We started a new mobile careers library last year.' The next question should be along the lines 'Tell us what your particular role was in this project.'

- Try to gain a picture of the candidate at work. Questions to help with this include: 'Describe a typical day's routine'; 'Tell us what contact you have with other staff in the course of your work'; 'What activities take up most of your time ... or do you find most interesting/difficult/ frustrating/rewarding?'

CV analysis

The use of application forms is almost universal. They provide information in a standardised form and can therefore be used to make a systematic, comparative analysis between candidates. It can be helpful to tabulate the main features—education, qualifications, type and length of experience—and allocate them a point score or weighting against the person specification. One management consultancy has developed this method into a sophisticated selection tool ('biodata' analysis) in which certain patterns of life histories are matched against success in certain types of work.

Reference enquiries

Many authorities ask candidates for the names of at least two referees and then seek written references from these sources. The practice is of doubtful value. No candidate is knowingly going to quote the source of an adverse reference. Most referees feel under some obligation to emphasise the candidate's positive rather than negative characteristics.

Of much more use is the telephone enquiry made direct to the candidate's current and previous manager. There may, of course, be good reasons for this approach not to be made to the present employer—and any such confidentiality about the application must be respected. Apart from this, though, managers should not feel inhibited from making direct enquiries, regardless of the names given by the candidate as formal referees.

Written tasks and presentational skills

Many managerial and professional jobs require an ability to write clearly, often in report form. This is a skill which can be assessed directly by setting the candidates a written task. Senior staff also often have to attend committee meetings to present and explain their reports. In selecting a new chief executive in 1994, a district council included a written and presentational task in the two-day selection programme. Candidates were given a week in advance of the interviews to write a report on: 'The organisational and service implications of the internal market.' They then had to present this paper to a panel of elected members and answer questions on it in the same way as they would be questioned on a council or committee report. The same authority sets a task of this kind for all its chief officer and deputy appointments, and many third-tier posts where report writing and committee presentations are significant functions. The task not only provides information about writing skills: the topics chosen also enable an assessment to be made of candidates' originality and clarity of thought, while the presentation to a panel provides evidence of verbal communication skills.

Other authorities set a shorter written task as part of a one- or two-day selection process. Candidates for an area office administrator's post, for example, are asked to compose a reply to a letter of complaint by a member of the public about delays in providing a requested service.

Group tasks

A group of short-listed candidates may be set a task to work on as a group under observation. This technique has been used extensively for officer selection in the armed services. It can indicate qualities such as initiative, determination and leadership ability, though is less effective in identifying candidates who perform best on their own.

It is certainly not a method to be embarked on lightly, and the nature of the group task should be directly relevant to the type of work involved in the vacancy. One city authority, selecting a chief executive, set the candidates the task of discussing a set issue of relevance to the city's situation. It was recognised that an important skill for the chief executive was to stimulate and guide constructive discussion in the chief officers' group. The task (in which the candidates took turns at leading) simulated this activity.

Designing and observing group tasks requires particular skills, particularly if artificial tasks are to be used because of the difficulty of simulating real life. Expertise in the technique can be bought in from some selection consultants, who will set up the exercise and guide managers in what to observe and how to interpret the results.

Tests

There is an enormous range of selection tests available to assess everything from finger dexterity for a difficult manual task to personality assessments for budding chief executives. All that can be done here is to indicate the main types of test and suggest that full use could be made of them in local government. They include:

- tests of manual skills, used particularly for craft or apprentice selection;
- various aptitude tests for particular types of work such as draughtsmanship, computer programming, statistical and clerical work;
- tests of intellectual capacity—of critical or analytical ability;
- personality assessments.

Except for tests of manual skills, most are described generically as psychometric tests, as they attempt some measurement of traits of mind or personality. It cannot be too strongly emphasised that such tests should never be designed or used by untrained managers or personnel officers. They are sensitive, complex tools which should always be validated by occupational psychologists (normally through the British Psychological Society) even though many are designed to be administered and interpreted by trained lay persons—normally the personnel officer.

Tests should also be used for specific purposes, not just for general interest. This is particularly the case with personality assessments. There seems little point in producing a personality analysis, for example, if little thought has been given to the personality characteristics which are most appropriate to the job in question. This implies that some study should be made of the characteristics of existing job-holders to see if any personality pattern correlates with high or low performance. To allay candidates' possible concern about such tests, it is also good practice to show them and explain the results, and to provide all necessary assurances about confidentiality.

Despite these cautionary points, the fact remains that tests can provide an extremely useful contribution to the whole selection process. They illustrate the main theme of this chapter—that selection should not be dependent on one interview, and should make use of an array of techniques to arrive at a final balanced conclusion.

Assessment centres

The term 'assessment centre' is used to describe a comprehensive selection programme in which all the techniques described above are used. This normally involves at least a two-day selection event in which, in addition to individual and panel interviews, a battery of tests and individual and group tasks, the candidates are given a tour of the authority and meet elected members (and probably their potential future colleagues) on an informal basis.

Follow-up

Whichever selection techniques are used, it is important to assess their relevance and how well they contribute to the assessment of candidates' suitability. The performance and characteristics of successful candidates should be reviewed once they are in the post, and the results compared with the predictions or indications derived from selection tests and assessments.

QUESTIONS ABOUT YOUR OWN AUTHORITY

- How much time is taken per candidate in selecting staff at various levels in the authority?
- Are job descriptions used (and up-dated) as the basis for selection?
- Are person specifications used?
- Are target areas for recruitment defined?
- Are applications monitored to check the effectiveness of advertising and other recruitment methods?
- Is advertising limited to narrow or conventional sectors?
- Have all interviewers been trained in interview techniques?
- What other methods than interviewing are used?
- Is any follow-up made to assess the effectiveness of selection methods and decisions?

5

Appraisal and development

KEY POINTS

- The quality of the human resource can be improved by positive managerial action to develop skills and abilities.

- Effective staff development needs to be based on the definition and assessment of performance.

- All types of performance appraisal include regular in-depth discussions between managers and their staff of how well jobs are being done and what action is needed to correct weaknesses and build on strengths.

- Effective appraisal requires a definition of work standards and objectives.

- Appraisals need to include (but not be restricted to) assessment of training needs and career potential.

- There is no one ideal appraisal method: the detail and degree of formality in a scheme needs to be suited to the authority's particular needs and style.

- Development action should not be limited to external training courses. Other methods include:
  —in-house courses;
  —planned work experience;
  —coaching and mentoring on the job;
  —distance learning;
  —study visits and secondments.

- Staff should also be encouraged to take responsibility for their own programmes of continuous self-development.

The performance of employees can be much more variable than that of plant or equipment. Over time, it can also improve or deteriorate. People learn by experience, and even if no positive action is taken to help new employees improve, most will raise their performance levels as they become more knowledgeable and discover for themselves ways of getting their jobs done more efficiently. But leaving performance improvement to chance has at least four serious shortcomings:

- Employees may eventually reach an acceptable standard but will take far longer to do so than if positive developmental action was taken.
- The standard which becomes the norm may well be below the level which could be achieved, given positive action.
- Employees' response to changes in the organisation's needs may be very slow.
- The performance of some employees will deteriorate as they lose interest or fail to adjust to changing circumstances.

Positive action to raise and maintain employees' standards of performance in their present jobs, and to develop the qualities required for the future, is one of the most vital management tasks.

The subject is not, however, one-sided. Employees as well as employers have an interest in attaining high standards, partly because of the personal satisfaction gained from work well done, partly because success in one job is a normal stepping stone to promotion. Employee development needs to be seen as a joint process in which manager and managed work together.

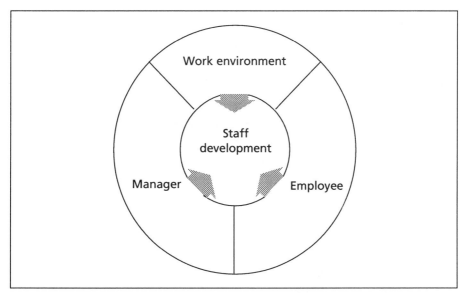

Figure 5.1 Influences on staff development

There are three main influences on an employee's development, and each has several components. This is shown diagrammatically in Figure 5.1.

- The influence of the whole work environment—starting with the style or culture of the organisation as a whole, but including also the impact of the immediate working group, the shape of the particular job, and the nature of the work.

- The influence of the manager, and this includes the quality of informal day-to-day contact, and more formal actions such as allocating a task in order to provide developmental experience or sending the employee on a training course.

- Self-development by the employee: stimulated by job interest or career ambition.

What the manager can do to optimise the development process is considered later in this chapter. It is necessary first to examine the assessment or appraisal of performance. Planned development must be directed—what it aims to achieve must be known and understood by both manager and employee—and this in turn implies that current and required performance standards require identification.

❏ Appraisal

As noted in Chapter 1, there has been a widespread introduction of appraisal schemes throughout local government since the mid 1980s. By 1994, most authorities were using some form of appraisal, though not always for all their staff. There has been a tendency to operate systematic appraisal more widely for managerial than other staff, and very few authorities yet include manual employees.

An Audit Commission study in 1994 also found that some authorities which had introduced appraisal schemes were not operating them effectively. For example, in the schemes studied, 30 per cent of the staff eligible for an annual performance review had not received an appraisal interview in the previous twelve months.

Managers with no experience of performance appraisal often say that they know their staff sufficiently well on an informal basis to make any formal system of assessment unnecessary. The experience of managers who operate a systematic approach throws serious doubt on such complacency. Most will say that it was only when they began to assess performance in a consistent way that they really obtained a full picture of all their staffs' strengths and weaknesses. Only when this full picture was available could they plan a programme of developmental action, both to improve current work performance and to develop employees' general competence.

At the heart of all good schemes is an in-depth discussion (usually annual) between manager and employee about how the job is being done. Measures to improve performance and the employee's capabilities are discussed and agreed. The process is two-way and the employee's involvement is of critical importance in securing commitment to subsequent action. If appraisal is left wholly to chance, these regular in-depth discussions about the whole job (past, present and future) will not occur. The manager may know quite a lot about the staff—but will they know what is thought of their performance, and will the manager know what they consider to be the barriers to, or opportunities for, improvement?

There are three main considerations in the design of an appraisal scheme:

■ Achieving a balance between targeting specific work tasks and objectives and the development of broader or more general competencies.

■ Using appraisal both to improve current performance and to identify employees' individual training and personal development needs.

■ Deciding the degree of formality or administrative detail.

Setting objectives

The first issue—objectives or competence—is one primarily of emphasis and in effective schemes this emphasis is balanced. At the two extremes, however, there is a significant difference.

In an approach based solely on objectives, an attempt is made each year to identify several key tasks or targets to be achieved in the course of the next 12 months. Most objective-oriented schemes also lean towards quantifiable targets wherever practicable. For example, two of the objectives for the DSO manager in one authority one year were:

■ to achieve a profit level of at least 7.5%;

■ to reduce the number of administrative staff from 27 to 21.

This example would be seen by some managers as illustrative of what they perceive as the major problem for appraisal in local government—the absence in many jobs of readily quantifiable objectives. It would be argued that a DSO manager is one of the very few jobs in which one financial index—profit—can be used as a primary indicator of performance. Narrowly, that is true; only trading organisations can use profitability as an objective. But there are many other ways of defining performance targets. Some examples drawn from two other authorities are:

- For an assistant personnel officer: to assess the value of using selection tests for trainee recruitment, and to report with costed recommendations by the end of June.

- For a senior accountant: to implement the revised system of monthly budget statements within the next four months, and to ensure that these statements are issued within five working days of the end of each accounting period.

- For a word-processing supervisor: to introduce a system of allocating priorities to reports awaiting processing, agreed with the chief administrative officers of 'client' departments, and to have this operating on a trial basis by 1 January.

All of these targets are capable of objective assessment—though in two cases (the report on tests and the priority system for word processing) subjective judgment will also be needed about their quality.

Competence

If the objectives approach concentrates on specific targets, an approach based on competencies looks at the employee's overall abilities to handle the totality of the job. This approach examines the characteristics of the job done well (or badly). There are two ways of looking at this:

- One is to take each element in the job description and consider how well it is being performed. Are any parts of the job proving particularly difficult, or being well done? What are the reasons for high or low performance? What action might be taken to put things right; or to use more fully particular skills which are being displayed?

- The other is to examine total performance against a series of criteria. Is the employee sufficiently knowledgeable to get the job done well? Is his or her output adequate in volume or timing? Are good relationships being maintained? Are there aspects of the employee's conduct or attitude which need attention?

To illustrate different approaches, examples can be used, drawn from schemes being operated by two authorities:

- In the first, the annual discussion with each employee begins with a check that the job description is still accurate. Employees and appraising managers are asked to review the job description before their discussions and to be ready to comment on any changes they think are necessary. At the discussion, the employee is asked:

  'What aspects of your job do you do best … and least well?'
  'What particular difficulties have you had with your job since the last review?'
  'How might these problems have been avoided by you or your manager?'
  'What have been the particular achievements in your work since the last review, assessed against last year's targets?
  'What specific tasks or targets should you work towards during the next review period?'

Managers are asked to bring to their discussions their own views of their employees together with proposals for new targets, and the ensuing discussions often usefully reveal (and resolve) very different perceptions between managers and their staff.

- In the second example, the employee's performance is assessed and discussed against headings, such as:
  Job knowledge
  Quality of work
  Quantity of work
  Relationships with management
  Relationships with the public
  Relationships with colleagues.

For each heading, a standard is defined for 'basically acceptable performance', 'significantly above basic' and 'outstanding performance'. Thus for a housing officer job which involves direct contact with the public, the three levels of performance under the heading 'relationships with the public' might be:

  Basic: able to deal with all routine enquiries correctly, but needs to refer difficult clients to supervisor. Manner with the public is acceptable, but is not remarked on by them as being other than what they expect.
  Significantly above basic: able to deal quickly and effectively with almost all enquiries, however difficult, and only rarely seeks assistance from supervisor. Manner quite often leads to unsolicited appreciative comments from clients.
  Outstanding: recognised by the department and clients as an expert in the subject matter of every enquiry, and in the highly effective and very pleasant manner adopted. The department receives many appreciative comments, even from difficult clients.

Improving performance

Some schemes, particularly those based on very specific objectives, concentrate almost entirely on raising standards of performance in the current job. Any consideration of staff training needs, or the identification of potential, are dealt with as a subsidiary issue. The advantage of this approach is that it promotes a very high level of performance consciousness.

The disadvantages are that employees may see the approach as one-sided, with no opportunity for their longer-term career ambitions to be considered: while it also fails to make full use of the appraisal discussion by omitting to consider how training or other developmental action might contribute to human resourcing needs.

Identifying training needs

A concentration solely on training needs has similar pros and cons. The highways' department of one authority operates a system of annual discussions with the professional staff, to identify what needs to be done to keep them up-to-date with developments in design theory, new materials and other technical matters. From these discussions, an annual programme of in-house seminars, outside visits and training-course attendances is evolved. The discussions do not consider individual performance, except to the extent that this is influenced by the level of technical know-how.

While this scheme is a very valuable way of maintaining the department's professional expertise, it does little to raise managerial performance and provides no opportunity for joint discussion between managers and their staff about individual standards of whole-job performance.

It is rare for schemes to be as training-centred as this. More common is the hybrid scheme in which training needs and work performance are both considered. Some such schemes may have been started with a training bias in order to overcome initial objections by staff or trade unions to performance assessment. There is often a considerable amount of suspicion when schemes are first mooted: staff may be afraid that the whole approach will be one of fault-finding. It can be extremely helpful in such circumstances to show that the scheme provides a mechanism for staff's own views about their training needs and career progression to be considered. Questions can be asked such as:

- What training have you had during the past year? Do you think it was of benefit?

- What training do you think you now need to help you do your job better?

- How do you wish your career to develop? What training do you think would help with this?

In any scheme which is strongly biased towards the identification of training and career development needs, there is a risk that employees may gain unrealistic expectations of promotion prospects. The most effective schemes strike a balance between targeting improvements in current job performance and reviewing longer-term employee development.

Formal and informal systems

A common question asked by managers about a proposed appraisal scheme is: what forms will we have to complete? It is a question which reveals a weakness of many schemes which pay too little regard to the fundamental purpose of appraisal and too much to the purely administrative aspect. If forms are to be used, then they should be seen as a helpful aid to achieving the objectives of the scheme and not as an end in themselves.

It is possible to be systematic about appraisal without using forms. One large authority set out such an approach in a 'practice note' to all its managers:

Every manager should set aside some time each year to talk individually to each of the staff he or she directly supervises. This can be done thus:

- set aside at least an hour for each employee;

- invite each employee to a discussion, asking them to give prior thought to:
  —any problems in the job
  —any ideas for improving the job
  —objectives for next year
  —career ambitions

- at the discussion, check all elements of the job and identify strong and weak points;

- discuss and clarify what results or standards are expected and how they are to be achieved;

- agree action (and by whom) to correct weaknesses or make better use of strengths, with deadlines;

- after the discussion, write a short note to the employee, summarising the key points discussed and the action programme;

- check at appropriate intervals during the year that this action is being implemented.

In a more formal approach, forms will be used to standardise the way in which the appraisal is conducted and recorded. It is normal for such forms to be signed by the appraisee, the appraising manager and that manager's senior. Completed forms may also be passed to the personnel officer so that training requirements can be extracted.

One large authority's scheme requires a six-page form to be completed of which the core is a list of 'principal accountabilities'. These are described as 'the enduring aspects of each job. They do not change unless the job itself changes, but their relative importance may vary from year to year to reflect service priorities, goals and programmes ...' Against each principal accountability, there are six columns to be completed.

- The relative importance of each accountability for the year, expressed as a percentage figure.

- A set of 'performance measures' to assess how well each accountability has been met. As far as possible, these measures are quantified.

- A set of 'performance and personal development goals' for the year. Performance goals are work targets; personal development goals include specified training plans.

- A note of 'assumptions'—that is, the basis on which the various measures and goals have been produced, such as a new service programme or priority.

- The 'agreed assessment' of last year's performance.

- 'Implications for the coming year' which includes a note of action to be taken by the appraiser as well as the appraisee.

Integrating appraisal with authority objectives

The highly structured scheme in the last example illustrates a key principle of human resource management—the integration of employee management practices with the authority's whole operational purpose and culture. The scheme of employee appraisal in this example is but one part of a total 'performance management system'. This starts with elected member involvement in the definition of service objectives, and includes procedures for monitoring service and departmental performance. In other words, individual appraisal flows down from a process of corporate objective setting and appraisal. It is not conducted as an isolated personnel procedure.

The detailed nature of this particular scheme is also consistent with the consciously adopted character or culture of the authority as a whole. The scheme would not be appropriate in an authority with a less structured or analytical style. But managers wishing to introduce appraisal schemes must start with an analysis of their authority's objectives, style and values, and tailor a scheme to fit. Buying in a scheme 'off the shelf' or copying a neighbouring authority's scheme is a recipe for failure.

❏ Training and development

Individual training and development needs which are identified through an appraisal process need to be set in the wider context of the needs for new skills which arise from externally driven changes and service plans. For example, one result of CCT has been the need for staff in the client function to develop new skills in the specification of contracts and the management of contractors: while the staff of in-house contractors or business units require commercial and marketing skills. Similarly, the care in the community policy has resulted in many changes of emphasis in social services work, with consequent changes in employees' training needs.

Whether drawn from individual or corporate appraisal, training and development requirements fall into three broad categories:

- The need for additional knowledge—for example, of new legislation or new techniques.

- The need for new or higher level skills—the practical or active application of knowledge to particular functions.

- The need for attitudinal change—for example, to understand and support the principles of equal opportunities or to become market-oriented.

The three elements interact. It is impossible to be fully skilful without adequate technical or professional know-how. Performance is vitally affected by attitude, which is influenced by the level of understanding or knowledge. To achieve developmental objectives, therefore, an array of measures needs to be applied, as some forms of development are better suited to one element than another. Reliance solely on one training mode (usually the formal training course) will not achieve all-round improvement.

Qualification training and NVQs

Training for professional qualifications is the main training tradition in local government and has been supported by most authorities for decades. It is popular with employees because it serves their long-term career interests and provides authorities with a highly knowledgeable professional workforce.

Its weaknesses need to be recognised. Qualification syllabuses meet the examination requirements of professional institutes, not the service needs of individual authorities. The priorities of these institutes may not coincide with the emphases which are needed within an authority at a particular point of time. However, the introduction of National Vocational Qualifications (NVQs) has gone some way towards ensuring a closer relationship between organisational needs and the career interests of the members of professional institutes. These institutes have revised, or are revising, their qualification and examination systems to meet NVQ principles and standards, a central feature of which is the attainment and assessment of competence in the work situation. New NVQs are also being introduced to cover all types of jobs from the most basic (NVQ level 1) to full professional and managerial work (NVQ level 5). Many local authorities are now using NVQs as a major element in their training and development programmes, with personnel and managerial staff being trained as NVQ assessors. Many authorities are also encouraging staff to develop a sense of ownership of their own development by making self-learning packages available and by the use of individual training logs in which employees record all their learning experiences.

External training courses

An enormous choice of courses is available through colleges, training organisations, regional employers' organisations and other external bodies. They range from the one-day seminar to top management courses of several weeks' duration.

Some are specific to local government, such as the Top Managers' Programme launched in 1994 by the LGMB. Others are on offer to all employers, providing local government delegates with the experience of mixing with private-sector staff.

These courses serve several purposes:

- The shorter courses concentrate mainly on imparting knowledge. Many authorities' staff, for example, have attended one- and two-day courses to learn about competitive tendering legislation. This will not of itself guarantee that these staff will display a high level of competence in managing the tendering process, but it will help to ensure that they avoid factual errors.

- Longer courses provide time for the development of skills, as well as imparting knowledge. Examples include courses in selection interviewing or in negotiation.

- The longest courses, limited almost entirely to senior management training, can combine the development of knowledge and skills. They can also help in changing attitudes, e.g. by providing the time for a lengthy reconsideration of the manager's role, in an environment conducive to in-depth personal study.

In-house courses

Most large authorities have their own training units which provide a variety of short internal training courses. The main advantage of in-house training is that training material can be drawn from the authority's own policies and experience, and be directly supportive of service objectives.

However, a reliance solely on in-house training will not provide the stimulus of external ideas. A mix of external and in-house courses is usually the best approach. Another variant is to retain external trainers (from a local college, for example) to run tailor-made courses in-house. External expertise can thus be put into a local setting and made relevant to the authority's particular needs.

Planned work experience

This is probably the least used, yet is potentially a very effective form of staff development. Most people learn more, and more quickly, from doing rather than listening. This natural learning process can be exploited if managers continually scan their departments' work programmes to identify opportunities to provide staff with practical learning experiences.

One authority has adopted this type of learning as the main method of management training, which it terms 'opportunistic development'. The aim is to combine task and training goals. Managers' training needs are identified through a normal appraisal process. For example, one manager may be assessed as needing to develop higher skills of verbal presentation. Instead of sending him or her to a training course in public speaking, the senior manager looks for a normal work opportunity which requires the verbal presentation of, say, a report to the chief officer's group. The officer under development is selected for this task and coached in what is required. Afterwards, his or her performance is discussed with further advice or coaching.

The opportunities for this form of coached on-the-job training are extensive— provided all managers keep development as well as task objectives in mind when allocating work to their staff.

Other forms of training

There are many other forms of training or development. Among them, in very brief terms, are:

- mentoring: in which an experienced colleague (not the trainee's manager) acts as a guide or tutor;

- distance learning: in which the employee follows a course of study using material provided by an external body (such as the Open University) or by an in-house training unit;

- study visits to other authorities and organisations;

- secondments to other authorities, or to the Civil Service or industry; or within an authority, to other departments;

- planned reading programmes;

- participation in inter-departmental study groups;

- 'management clubs': in which managers organise their own programmes of events such as visits and lunchtime talks by outside speakers;

- involvement in the activities of professional bodies or other external organisations to acquire experience not available in-house.

❏ Continuous- and self-development

If one aim of human resource management is to stimulate initiative and commitment, then one aspect of training is to encourage employees to take a large measure of responsibility for their own development. The management role is to provide a working environment in which development is facilitated, but employees 'own' the personal learning process.

To quote one authority's management guide to self-development: 'Development cannot be applied to someone from the outside; it is a process which has to be driven from within. ... The most the authority can do is to provide the conditions and processes in which each employee's own learning effort can be most effective.'

Self-development principles can apply to all levels of staff, but are particularly relevant for chief officers. They are the providers of training or training resources for their staff—but who trains and develops them? One answer is themselves, by being systematic about the identification of their own training needs and the production of their own personal training plans.

For example, in one authority which encourages chief officers to commit themselves to annual development plans, the chief planning officer's plan for 1994 was:

- to study privately for the Open Business School course, 'Managing People';
- to learn how to use the Internet;
- to visit at least four other authorities to discuss how they were responding to the new building control regulations.

This example illustrates that development should be seen as a continuous process. No one ever exhausts the need or opportunities for learning. As the Institute of Personnel and Development's code says on this subject: 'continuous development is self-directed, lifelong learning ... not a series of short term expedients'.

This theme of continuity should apply, too, to the corporate side of staff development. Just as individual employees have on-going development needs throughout their working lives, so the authority (and every manager within it) should consider training and development as being an integral and continuous element in the planning and implementation of authority and service policies. Formal appraisal may occur only once a year, but this should be a stock-take of where things are within a continuous process—not the only time each year that training and development are thought about.

QUESTIONS ABOUT YOUR OWN AUTHORITY

- Do staff know what standards and objectives they are expected to attain?

- Do all managers discuss performance regularly with each of their staff and agree consequent action?

- Are such discussions set within some form of systematic scheme or process?

- How are individual and collective training needs identified? Are training programmes evolved and budgeted?

- Is training limited to formal qualification courses? Or to attendance at off-the-job courses?

- Is any systematic use made of planned work experience and other work-based development?

- Are staff helped to evolve and follow their own self-development programmes?

- Is training seen as a one-off event, or as continuous development?

6

Staff motivation

KEY POINTS

- How well people work is influenced as much by attitude and motivation as by competence.

- Motivation is affected by an amalgam of influences—personal, job-related, environmental and managerial.

- Managers need to understand each employee as a unique individual.

- Jobs need to be meaningful and interesting, and people need feedback on their performance.

- Work needs to be seen as partially a social process, and motivation is affected by group attitudes.

- An organisation's general culture has a strong motivational influence.

- Motivation can be stimulated by effective systems of recognition and reward.

- Managerial leadership is vital: there is no one leadership style, but qualities such as consistency, commitment, fairness, decisiveness and communication are common factors.

Even a well-trained employee may not work well. Within a group of staff who are all technically competent, some may be outstandingly high performers while others may be barely satisfactory. People's behaviour at work is variable, and the reasons for this are complex. The ideal situation, of course, is when all employees perform at the same high level, but the rarity of this occurrence emphasises the importance managers need to place on staff motivation. The simple question is: what makes people work well?

There are two sets of factors involved: one concerned with the personal characteristics of the employee, one with the situation in which the employee works. Motivation is all about the interaction between an employee and the work, and the extent to which the employee's personal needs, values and drives are satisfied by the working experience. To examine this from a practical management viewpoint, a more detailed categorisation of factors is needed:

- factors relating to the individual employee;
- factors concerning the job;
- the effect of the work environment—physical, social and cultural;
- systems of recognition, reward and sanction;
- the style and behaviour of the employee's manager.

❏ The employee

There is not single set of personal characteristics which makes up the highly self-motivated employee. Achieving a motivated workforce is not just a matter of selecting employees of one particular personality type. Each employee has a personal set of characteristics and values which influence the degree of motivation in any particular set of circumstances. The starting point for any manager who aims to achieve a highly motivated workforce must be an understanding of the individual and therefore differing characteristics of each employee. The main features to consider are:

- Personal circumstances. There is no rigid separation between employees' behaviour at work and their personal or domestic life. Thus the features in a job which motivate the head of a one-parent family may be very different from those of a single person with no domestic responsibilities.

- Personal interests. The extent to which a person's work coincides or conflicts with their interests outside the job can be a significant factor. In some cases, the outside interests compensate for boredom at work; for other people, the job may be the most satisfying part of their lives. Sometimes, the two coincide. In one authority's museums service, for example, the keeper of ceramics is herself a nationally known private collector and enthusiast—job and private interest being wholly coincident.

- Intellectual capacity. There is an interaction between a person's intellectual capacity and the intellectual stimulus or demands of the job. A high level of motivation cannot be expected if there is a major mismatch. Stress will arise from a failure to cope with the demands of the job; boredom will be generated if the work is too limited in its intellectual challenge.

- Personality factors. There are many aspects of personality which can influence motivation. A highly extroverted or sociable employee is unlikely to perform well in an isolated job. A person with a strong competitive drive works best in a challenging environment. The careful, cautious, analytical personality is best suited to work involving close attention to detail and precision.

For managers, the requirement is to know each employee well and so to understand the individual characteristics which are likely to influence each person's motivation.

❑ The job

The phrase 'job satisfaction' has been widely used in management literature. There is a general assumption that people need to gain a sense of achievement from their work and that there are certain characteristics of job design which can achieve this. Because people vary so much as individuals, the adoption of one standard model is dangerous—not all employees will respond favourably, for example, to the type of job which maximises personal responsibility.

Nevertheless, there are some general points which can at least be used as a checklist when deciding how best to structure work into jobs.

- Variety of tasks. Many (though not all) employees will comment favourably about their work if it provides some variety of action and the consequent exercise of more than one skill. Mass-production word processing is an example of a job lacking this variety. Could it be made more interesting and, therefore, more motivating by introducing some filing or telephone work? More generally, is a flow process, with each employee in a section handling just one element in a total transaction, the most satisfying work pattern? Is it possible for each employee to handle a whole transaction and so be able to use a range of skills? A number of authorities have redesigned their jobs in front offices so that employees taking enquiries from the public take responsibility for finding the answers and replying, instead of just passing the enquiry on to another office.

- Wholeness of task. The example just quoted also illustrates that many people find jobs more satisfying if they involve the completion of complete pieces of work. This is not just a matter of variety—it is the sense of achievement which comes from producing an identifiable whole outcome.

- Significance. Few people gain much satisfaction from doing jobs which either seem to be unimportant or in which their significance is unknown. In any well-designed organisation, all jobs are essential—otherwise they would not be there—but do all employees understand the importance of the contribution their particular jobs make to the authority's objectives and services?

- Responsibility and autonomy. How closely is the job prescribed? What scope is there for the employee to exercise discretion and make decisions? How closely is the work monitored or checked? The general trend in job design is empowerment—giving the individual employee more autonomy—to generate a sense of responsibility by giving more responsibility, for example, by making employees responsible for quality checking their own work, rather than making this a separate inspection task. There is little doubt that many people respond positively to this approach. It does need to be kept in mind, however, that employees vary in their intellectual and personality characteristics and, consequently, vary in the extent to which they will happily take on more responsibility.

- Feedback. No one enjoys working in a vacuum. Everyone (including chief officers and chief executives) needs to know whether their work is achieving desired results. 'Tell me how I'm doing', is a universal question, even if not all employees are bold enough to ask it directly. Jobs themselves can have feedback mechanisms built into them: it is not just a matter of appraisal systems. One of the major functions of any management information system, for example, is the provision of data to enable managers to monitor and correct their own performance.

The conversion of work processes into interesting individual jobs is consequently a most important element in human resource management. By recognising that work is generally best done when jobs are 'people-shaped' rather than designed as though they were parts of a machine process, it makes the fullest possible use of the innate human characteristics of adaptability, flexibility, imagination, creativity and enthusiasm. Every employee is different and will respond differently to different work patterns, but none is a machine.

❏ The work environment

Although the shape of the individual job is of major importance, jobs do not exist in isolation. They exist in physical, social and cultural settings which all influence the motivational climate.

Physical environment

This factor can be used to illustrate the negative aspect of motivation. There are some factors which positively stimulate a high level of employee commitment and performance. Others—and the physical environment is one—are important more for their demotivating effect if things are wrong. To quote from one authority's guidance notes to managers on employee motivation:

> *Uncomfortable seating, poor lighting, a drab office—all these can contribute to a depressing environment not conductive to the generation of employee enthusiasm. It would be a mistake, however, to claim too much positive value from an attractive working environment. This factor, if conditions are poor, is more important as a de-motivator than are good conditions as a major and positive aid to high motivation.*

That said, it should nevertheless be recognised that poor physical working conditions can have a severely depressing effect on staff morale and performance. Local authority standards are extremely variable, ranging from superb modern offices designed by ergonomic and interior design consultants, to some of the most drab, overcrowded and poorly equipped offices ever likely to be found.

Social environment

All jobs involve some interaction between employees, so that work itself is partially a social process. The social environment, though, is wider than this. Employees work in teams or groups—formal and informal—and these groups tend to develop their own style, beliefs and values. The psychological pressure to conform to group norms is very strong, and if these norms conflict with those of the organisation, the probability is that the individual employee will be influenced more by the group. A district council experienced this when confrontational relationships developed between the client unit of its leisure services department and the commercial leisure contractor. The authority's policy was for client/contractor relationships to be collaborative. However, staff attitudes in the client unit were influenced by resentment about changes to their original contract specification made by a members' panel which had led to the contract being awarded externally. Group pressure to adopt an aggressive, fault-finding attitude towards the contractor over-rode the authority's policy aims.

Less dramatic, but similarly influential, are the unofficial group standards which can evolve about acceptable levels of effort or work quality. Where individually measured bonus schemes are operated, for example, it is not unusual for the work group to let new employees know that to go beyond a certain level of output is considered unfair to the group as a whole. The fear is probably that if one or two employees demonstrate that it is possible to sustain a much higher performance than normal, management will revise the targets upwards.

Managers must be aware of these group influences and do all they can to ensure that, by a process of explanation, discussion and effective leadership, the values and norms of the group are as close or consistent as possible to those of the department or the authority. High levels of motivation cannot be expected from individual employees unless the work group as a whole is interested, committed and enthusiastic about the achievement of authority objectives.

Cultural environment

Groups as well as individuals work within the context of the organisation as a whole and are consequently strongly influenced by the authority's overall characteristics or culture. The concept of culture is dealt with in Chapter 3 and does not need to be repeated here. What needs emphasis in relation to motivation, however, is the strength of influence of culture on employee attitudes, conduct and performance.

Just as a poor physical environment can be demotivating, so can some cultural characteristics positively discourage employees from exercising initiative, effort and imagination. Two particular features of this kind are:

- A managerial emphasis on fault-finding and on intolerance of mistakes. Obviously, inaccurate or poor-quality work cannot be allowed to pass unnoticed; but if the whole managerial emphasis is placed on the avoidance of error rather than on service achievement, employees will soon learn that the safest way to survive is by sticking to the book, keeping a low profile, and avoiding anything new because it is more likely to generate a mistake than traditional methods and ideas. Wise managers use mistakes as a valuable learning experience, not as a reason for employee sanctions.

- An over-emphasis on administrative perfection for its own sake. There is strong administrative tradition in the public services which sometimes dominates the way things are done. Producing exhaustive minutes, filing every document, however ephemeral, insisting on written records of every transaction, however minor, producing complex and precise statistics when all that is needed is an indication of general trends— these are all common symptoms of over-administration. It is a style which can quickly erode flair and creativity, and demotivate the employee whose real interest is in responsive and sympathetic service to the public. Its antithesis is encapsulated by a motto which one county architect (with an international reputation for high-quality design) hangs on his office wall: 'The product, not the process!'

The introduction of the concept of the internal market is having a particularly powerful impact on organisational culture and managerial attitudes. It introduces formalised trading relationships (i.e. between client and contractor units) in place of previous informal, colleague-to-colleague contacts. The result can be the development of a confrontational cultural style between managers in these two roles. A great deal of effort and skilled leadership is required from the chief executive and the top management team to prevent this occurring and to build a partnership culture which recognises the value of role distinctions, but encourages each to work together for the benefit of the corporate whole. The key to evolving a motivational culture is the definition, explanation and promotion of a small number of key ideas or values. Thus for one authority, a key word is 'opportunistic'—taking advantage of every opportunity to try out new ideas, exploit new sources of funds, develop useful working contacts with other agencies, to innovate and experiment. By building this one word into the collective consciousness of the whole workforce, every employee is encouraged to apply this approach to his or her own job.

Other authorities emphasise different qualities or values, depending on their political perspectives and preferred styles and objectives. The common factor is not one particular culture, but the clarity of definition of the required characteristics, and the extent to which elected members and managers actively promote these qualities and objectives.

❑ Systems of recognition and reward

The idea that a high level of motivation can be stimulated by the provision of direct incentives is centuries old. Piecework payments pre-date the industrial revolution. In its crudest form, the theory is one of carrot and stick: produce well and be paid well, produce poorly and be sacked. If reality was as simple as the theory, all pay would be related directly to performance, and dismissals for poor performance would be commonplace. Neither is the case, and the debate on the pros and cons of performance-related pay continues unabated.

Incentive payment schemes

There is no doubt that many incentive schemes have failed to achieve the results expected of them. Employees operate unofficial output limits, schemes become administratively complex and expensive to operate, bonus targets become the subject of industrial disputes, employees who fail to reach performance payment levels become demotivated instead of striving to do better. The concepts of human resource management can provide some clues as to why conventional incentive schemes often produce such disappointing results.

As was emphasised in Chapter 1, employee management systems are most effective when they are integrated with the total management process, and support or are consistent with an organisation's culture and objectives. To date, however, too many incentive schemes have been designed as an end in themselves, without regard for the organisational, managerial and social setting in which they have to operate. Too many, also, constitute the only attention which management appears to give to performance appraisal.

For example, one authority operated a scheme in which staff were assessed annually as working at four levels of performance—below average, average, significantly above average, and outstanding. Performance increments were paid for the top two levels, and withdrawn if performance fell. Assessments were made by a panel consisting of the chief executive, the relevant chief officer and the personnel officer. The authority had no published strategic objectives, and there were no annual statements of what each department or section was trying to achieve (other than stay within budget). There was no system of annual appraisal discussions between manager and managed, and no staff development policy or programme. Neither was there any definition as to the performance characteristics which constituted the various levels used for payment purposes.

This is an extreme case of a payment system being operated in isolation from almost every factor which is needed to make such a system a success. The assessments were being made by managers who could not have a detailed day-to-day knowledge of how every employee worked. Employees had no information about the characteristics of good and poor performance. There were no generally understood values or objectives against which employees and managers could measure their own personal performance. There was no system of developmental support to help low achievers improve. The scheme drifted into an unofficial method of extending incremental pay scales with almost all staff eventually being classified as above average, but was eventually disbanded.

Schemes in authorities which have made a success of performance-related pay share the following characteristics:

- Payment schemes supplement a systematic and thorough form of performance appraisal, involving dialogue and agreement between manager and managed.

- Performance requirements are clearly specified, either as annual targets or as standing characteristics.

- These individual targets or standards are consistent with, and reinforce, wider departmental or authority objectives or values.

- Performance assessments are made by each manager about the staff reporting directly to them, subject only to checking by more senior managers.

- Low performers are given training and other assistance to improve— they are not treated as being penalised.

- At least 50% of staff become eligible for some form of payment; payments are not restricted to that small minority of exceptional performers who are so self-motivated that they would work at this level regardless of any direct incentive.

Performance payments in these schemes may be of two types:

- One-off lump sums, normally paid for the completion to a high standard of specific pieces of work.

- Additional salary increments, normally linked to sustained good performance across the whole job.

Some authorities use both types of payment in order to distinguish clearly between these two different aspects of high performance.

Although some authorities are satisfied that performance-related pay (PRP) is beneficial, its introduction merits very careful consideration. In a 1994 report *Paying the piper* the Audit Commission said: 'There is no clear evidence in the private or public sector that PRP improves employee motivation or performance', and concluded: 'Each authority must decide for itself whether the potential benefits of PRP outweigh the disadvantages.'

PRP is probably best thought of as a form of recognition of good performance, with the act of recognition being the primary motivator rather than the money. There is some evidence from the private sector that money alone motivates only when the PRP element is a large proportion of total pay— probably at least 25%. Local authorities can rarely afford to make performance related payments of more than 5%—so the motivational impact of the money alone is often minimal. However, personal thanks given for good performance, coupled with the presentation of a cheque (even for a very small sum) which is explained as a token of appreciation may well have significant motivational effect.

One danger in PRP is to link payments too directly to just one element of performance—often something which lends itself to statistical measurement but omits less quantifiable but still important qualititative aspects. To the extent that PRP can influence an employee's effort, it is only natural for most effort to be devoted to whatever generates the greatest financial reward. PRP can consequently distort performance if it fails to reflect the real performance priorities.

Other schemes

Two other types of scheme or system are in use in some authorities, both illustrating the theme of integration with authority objectives and values. One is a new approach to the conventional suggestion scheme; the other is based on the originally Japanese system of quality circles.

■ Conventional suggestion schemes rarely produce much employee interest. A few authorities have tried, successfully, to generate much better results by running quite short campaigns, during which employees are encouraged to submit ideas on a particular theme—not necessarily just to suggest measures to achieve savings. These themes tie in with ideas or values the authority wishes to promote in a wider context. Two examples are: An authority, which was launching a drive to make its services more responsive to the public, ran a four-month campaign in which employees were invited to submit ideas for improving service to the public. Prizes included a holiday for two and a video-recorder, and the whole campaign was conducted in a lively manner with professionally designed posters, pay-slip messages and talks by managers to explain the scheme. Another authority ran a similarly publicised campaign to support its energy conservation programme. Again, the campaign was given maximum publicity through the staff news-sheet, posters and a personal letter from the chairman, and culminated with a prize-giving event in the Town Hall, linked to a 'Save It' buffet and dance.

- Quality circles in industry consist of small work groups meeting regularly to discuss how they can improve their work output or quality standards. They have not been adopted to any significant degree in UK local government, but some authorities do encourage managers and supervisors to hold frequent, short meetings with their work teams to discuss work progress, problems and plans. In one DSO, for example, each highways superintendent spends about half an hour each Monday morning telling the team of roadworkers about the previous week's output and costs, describing the programme for the coming week, and seeking the employees' views and suggestions about improving productivity and quality. The essence of this process is its frequency—it needs to be seen as a normal part of the whole working routine—and the involvement of every single employee. It is a management practice which could be used much more extensively, and which private-sector experience shows can do much to develop employee interest and commitment.

❏ The role of the manager

This last example also demonstrates that the influence of the individual manager is of crucial importance. Whatever the wider organisational context, however intrinsically interesting the job is, and however well selected and trained the employee, that person's manager can still extinguish motivation by thoughtless or unskilled people management.

There are many processes or mechanisms which the manager can use to foster motivation, such as appraisal schemes. But none of these processes will operate to full effect without general, positive, managerial leadership. This does not imply that there is one best leadership style. The stereotype of the 'born leader' implies a highly charismatic personality—energetic, extrovert, enthusiastic and dominant. A few managers may naturally fit this pattern, but many do not, and it would be most unwise for them to try to copy it. Observation, too, will soon show that some managers who are excellent leaders are quiet, thoughtful and undemonstrative.

Ideal leadership qualities also vary in different circumstances. In a crisis, what may be needed is rapid, confident, but assertive decision-making. When long-term plans are being evolved for some new service development, the key quality may be the ability to stimulate new thinking in a team, and assist each team member to make a constructive contribution. The search for a single leadership model can be positively harmful. Yet if employees are asked about the qualities they most respect and expect in a good manager, six common factors emerge:

■ Competence. Employees respect a manager who is obviously an expert in his or her professional field. This does not mean that managers should be able to do all the jobs of all their employees: it does mean that they need to display a high level of competence in their own 'trades'.

■ Consistency. Employees need to know where they stand with their managers. Managers who blow hot and cold, who are friendly one day and aloof the next, who are unpredictable or variable about work standards, will find it difficult to gain their employees' confidence and respect.

■ Commitment. It is too much to expect employees to show enthusiasm and commitment to the authority's and departmental objectives, and to high productivity and quality, if they cannot see this commitment in their managers.

■ Fairness. Employees are very sensitive to any actual or apparent unfairness in the way they are treated. Any indication of favouritism, for example, in the allocation of interesting or rewarding work will rapidly undermine a manager's standing and demotivate otherwise enthusiastic employees.

■ Decisiveness. This quality does not imply that all managers at all times should be making quick, positive decisions. There are circumstances when the manager needs to hold back and encourage ideas and proposals for action to emerge from the work group or from individual employees. But there comes a point in most managerial processes or episodes when the manager needs to determine what is to be done. When that point is reached, employees appreciate firm, clear decisions. This is of particular importance if the decision has to be unpleasant. Wrapping up unpopular decisions in so convoluted a manner that employees are not sure what has been decided is a sure way, in the longer run, to lose employee respect. Part of an employee's tribute to one respected manager at his retirement event was 'He knew how to say no!'

- Communication. Well-informed employees are far more likely to display motivation than those left in the dark. The subject is dealt with fully in Chapter 7, but here it needs to be noted that one important channel of communication lies in the day-to-day working contacts between managers and their staff. Employees respect a manager who puts them in the picture about the authority as a whole, about the aims and activities of their department, and about their own work and its place in the scheme of things.

All six characteristics can be displayed in different ways by managers of very different personalities. What is important in leadership is not the superficiality of behaviour in terms of acting a part, but a sincerity of interest in employees' needs, and a consistency of content and purpose in managerial action.

QUESTIONS ABOUT YOUR OWN AUTHORITY

- Is the workforce committed and enthusiastic?
- Has thought been given to the design of jobs to make them interesting and worthwhile?
- Do some groups or teams have negative attitudes which inhibit individual initiative?
- Does the general culture of the authority encourage a high level of employee commitment?
- Is good performance demonstrably recognised—or is it only failure which attracts managerial attention?
- Are any positive methods used to reward initiative and high performance?
- Do managers understand the importance of effective leadership, and are they helped to develop their leadership abilities?

7
Communication

KEY POINTS

- An organisation is held together by effective communication.

- Employees need information about the purpose of their jobs, and about the policies, plans and values of their authority.

- Communication is a two-way process; managers need to listen to the views of employees.

- There are many communication modes—verbal, written; formal, informal. Message and mode need to be matched.

- To be effective, employee communication must be regular, honest, open and relevant.

Human resource management aims to achieve a committed workforce: that is, employees who individually and collectively have a sense of responsibility and pride in their work, and who are interested in and enthusiastic about the effective delivery of the services in which they are employed. Chapters 4, 5 and 6 have emphasised the contribution of effective selection, training and leadership to the development of such commitment, and it is important to recognise that every aspect of employee management has an impact on employee interest and morale.

There is, however, one element which permeates the whole array of employment measures—communication. A local authority, as any organisation, is held together by a network of formal and informal channels of information and communication. Managers need to relate to each other. The workforce at large needs direction and explanations from management. Management needs to understand the interests and concerns of the workforce. The more open these channels are, and the freer the flow of information, views and ideas within them, the greater is the likelihood of everyone in the organisation sharing the same interest and understanding of their common purpose.

The converse is also true. How can the workforce be expected to understand and support the authority's goals if these objectives and values have not been communicated? How can managers in different services co-ordinate their activities to achieve a consistent style or standard without effective communication between them. How can ill-informed employees (or managers, or elected members) effectively fulfil their proper roles?

This chapter examines the three main features of effective communication:

- the nature of the communication process—its three components of sender, medium and receiver;

- the content of communication—who needs to know what;

- communication modes.

❏ The communication process

In essence, every form of communication starts with an originator or sender who has a message (information, an idea, a request, an instruction) which, to be effective, has to be transmitted without distortion to a receiver. The process is illustrated by Figure 7.1.

At the macro level, the sender may be the council as a corporate body, wishing to inform all employees (the receivers) of, say, a newly defined equal opportunity policy. At the other end of the scale, and on a day-to-day basis, is the individual manager telling a single employee about the work target for

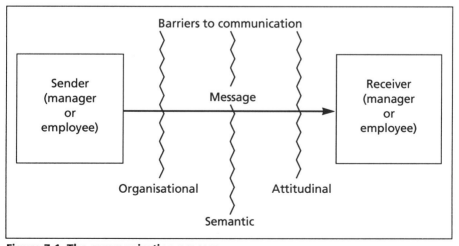

Figure 7.1 The communication process

the week; or the employee wishing to relay to the manager an idea for improving the efficiency of the job.

All three elements in the process can influence its effectiveness, and there are a number of potential barriers to successful communication:

- The sender may lack any real commitment to providing the message or information. Managers who communicate only with reluctance—perhaps questioning employees' 'right to know'—will probably fail to shape or deliver their communications well. Further, their reluctance will be detected by employees, who will then be suspicious about the managers' motivation and doubtful about the credibility of his or her messages.

- The communication process may lead to distortion of the message. This is particularly true of word-of-mouth messages passed down through several tiers of management and supervision before reaching the bulk of employees. Unwittingly, each person or tier in the communication chain will introduce their own emphasis or interpretation, and the final version of the message may bear little resemblance to what the originator said. Communication chains need to be as short as possible.

- The message may be in the wrong 'language'. Thus if employees are to be kept informed about the council's budgetary position, the message needs to be cast in everyday lay terms and not in accountants' jargon. One authority issued a budget leaflet to employees which spoke of 'regressive grant penalties'. After adverse comments from the trade unions, a new version was written by the public relations officer which explained that 'for every extra pound we spend we will lose almost £1.50 in government grant'. Communicators need always to think about the need for, and capacity of, the recipients to understand. Messages need to be in the recipients' language—not the sender's.

- Attitudinal barriers to communication do not stem only from direct lack of trust between sender and receiver. The whole climate of employer/employee relations has an effect. If an authority's normal style is formal and hierarchical, the sudden issue of a chatty staff bulletin with cartoon drawings and a message from the chief executive signing himself as Wilf would probably be met with derision and misbelief. Like all other aspects of human resource management, communication style and modes need to fit the total organisational and managerial culture.

- Communications which are not perceived as relevant are given little attention or are misunderstood. Relevance involves both subject matter and timeliness. Examples can be drawn from the way different authorities communicated with staff about the 1993–95 Local Government Review. Several authorities issued frequent staff newsletters, giving the latest information about the Commission's activities, but giving particular emphasis to details about the Staff Commission's proposals for staff transfers and compensation terms. This did much to reassure staff that they were being kept fully informed about issues of great concern. Some other authorities made no special effort to keep staff informed, and when information was given, the emphasis was on the disagreements between county and district objectives—not on the more detailed staffing implications which were worrying the workforce. In addition, staff read about the county/district issues in the local press long before having any information from their authorities.

❏ The content of communication

Who needs to know what? That is the question lying behind the design of any communication strategy, and it can be answered fully only by each authority examining its own needs at particular points in time. It is certainly not a matter of telling everybody everything: superfluity in communication can be almost as serious a flaw as inadequacy. There are, though, some general principles.

Very broadly, employees' information needs fall into two categories:

- Information relating to the individual: the purpose and demands of the job, pay and conditions of service, training and career opportunities, rules and regulations, employment and work procedures.

- Information about the authority: the function of the section, department or service, the authority's standards and values, the organisation structure and who's who within it, service and authority plans, problems and policies.

In the first category, it is particularly important that new employees are helped to integrate quickly by a planned programme of induction which should start with information of immediate, practical concern. Employees on their first day want to know the basic things about where the lavatories and canteen are, how to record their attendance, and who their supervisor is—not what the long-term strategic policies are of the authority as a whole. That can come later.

The purpose of providing authority information is threefold:

- To help the individual employee understand the relevance of his or her job to the total function or purpose of the service.

- To create a commonality of interest and understanding about the authority's priorities and values, so that individual employees make decisions and generally conduct themselves in a way which reinforces the authority's objectives.

- To contribute to the authority's external image by every employee being able to act as an ambassador for the authority within the wider community.

Communication is not, however, only a one-way process from management of the council to the workforce. The authority has a need—even if it is not always recognised—to know about the hopes, fears and ideas of employees at large. Formally, much of this information is channelled through the trade unions who can act as the collective voice of the workforce. But there is a need to go beyond this. All managers need to listen to their own staff and thus to communicate directly with all—not just through the union representatives. Shop stewards are placed in an inappropriate position if they are expected by managers to take responsibility for relaying managerial information.

Managers also need to communicate with each other. Analyses of the time managers spend in different types of contact often show that far longer is spent in sideways relationships with managers and specialists in other sections or services, than in hierarchical working with seniors or subordinates. The quality of these horizontal contacts is of crucial importance, and is affected to a major degree by the effectiveness of the communication modes used.

❑ Communication modes

The choice of modes of communication is continually increasing. In the last century the choice was limited to the written word or face-to-face verbal communication. The telephone was the first major additional business facility. Within the last decade, there has been a communication explosion and the choice now includes the latest technological developments of interactive video and electronic mail.

While this expansion of choice makes effective communication easier to achieve—if properly planned—it also carries the danger of using the wrong medium for the wrong message. For example, one local authority's personnel department was supplied with computer terminals for each of the eight members of the management team, as well as for one in three of the other staff of the department. One facility of this network was internal electronic mail. Enthused by this technology, several members of the management team began to use electronic messages for almost all their contacts with their colleagues and other staff. The chief personnel officer had to intervene to encourage a reversion to the previous, and more effective, habit of direct, informal personal contact—talking to each other.

It is therefore worth examining the various communication media and their generally most effective uses.

Talking to individuals

Face-to-face conversation is the most natural and consequently most effective method of communication for most purposes, provided that it is logistically possible. In a two-person business it is doubtful if any other method is ever used except when documents are necessary, either for legal purposes or to provide a record of complicated data. Local authorities of course, are not two-person businesses, and it is impossible for the chief executive or most chief officers to relate to the staff by reliance solely on conversational contact.

The power of such direct contact cannot, however, be over-emphasised. Talking with staff enables managers to check whether their instructions or messages have been understood, to rephrase or add explanations to achieve this understanding, to listen to employees' ideas and to answer their questions. In manager-to-manager contact, talking together will often smooth out differences of view which correspondence by memo might well exacerbate, and will reveal underlying attitudes which explain why differences exist. The interaction in a discussion will also stimulate new thinking and enable solutions or ideas to emerge which other communication modes would never generate.

Talking to small groups

The larger the group, the less easy it is to achieve active interaction between the group leader and group members. Nevertheless, one very effective form of communication with employees is the small 'briefing group' (to use the phrase promoted by the Industrial Society who advocate this method). Briefing groups are used extensively in some companies and to a growing extent by some local authorities. They could almost certainly be used more.

The principle is that each manager or supervisor holds a short meeting at regular and frequent intervals (probably weekly) with all the staff who report directly to them. This usually limits the numbers to between about six and fifteen. A larger group would make individual participation in any discussion difficult. Briefing meetings take no more than half an hour. Managers are provided with briefing notes of any news about the organisation as a whole which they can then relay to their groups. They also comment on current work problems and plans, explain any new objectives, and ask for comments and questions.

To be effective, briefing groups must become part of the normal working routine, be held at set times, and occur frequently. Managers need some basic training in how to conduct a group session of this kind—particularly if it is not to become a managerial monologue—and be provided with a regular supply of interesting and relevant news about the authority.

Mass meetings

Occasionally, it may be helpful for senior management to address much larger gatherings of employees. For example, the leader and chief executive in one small district council make an annual presentation to a general meeting of all staff in the town hall to explain the next year's budget. This is used as an opportunity not just to deal with the authority's financial position, but also to promote service policies and values.

Size, of course, influences the practicability of such meetings, and no county council could convene a meeting attended by all staff. Mass meetings, too, are inevitably one-way affairs—there is little scope for employees to respond to the managerial message.

Joint consultation

Many aspects of formal joint consultative systems lie outside the scope of this chapter, being concerned more with the conduct of relationships between the authority and the trade unions than with communications *per se*.

Nevertheless, joint consultative committees do provide one important channel for two-way management/employee communication, while the wide circulation of their minutes can also form part of an authority's system of documentary employee information.

From a communications viewpoint, conventional 'JCC's' often have several serious flaws:

- The subject matter of their agendas is often limited to minor issues such as the quality of the canteen tea, or to problems about the detail of, say, overtime allocations or payment systems.

- Managers often leave to union representatives the task of relaying management or authority information to the workforce at large.

- The minutes of these meetings are often written in flat, jargon-ridden prose and as a result are read by very few employees.

For JCC's to operate as an effective communication channel, they need to be used as a regular means of explaining and discussing important developments in an authority's service plans and priorities. Their minutes can be written in a more journalistic style, attractively produced and widely distributed. Managers should not, however, rely solely on this channel for keeping employees informed about important work or service issues. There is no good substitute for the briefing group approach, which involves all employees, not just union representatives.

Newsletters or magazines

A number of authorities produce staff magazines or news-sheets, varying from the duplicated typed letter to highly professional magazines in either journal or newspaper format.

There must be doubt as to whether unattractive formats, often with poorly drafted contents, do any good at all. At worst, they may give employees the impression that the authority has little real concern for their information needs, and has an unimaginative, mean-minded or boring management. The advice which any professional communicator will give is that staff magazines need to be well designed and skilfully written if they are to make any real impact. They are also of limited value if they are produced very infrequently. They are certainly not something which a busy personnel department should be expected to produce as a sideline and without professional media help.

Their style and content also need careful consideration. Too often, they include only what the authority considers good news, together with endless accounts of retirement parties, written in a tediously forced jocular vein. To quote from an IPM study (*Practical Participation and Involvement,* IPM, 1981):

> *For a works paper to be an effective means of communication it has to build the credibility which only comes with a willingness to carry unpalatable truths and criticism ... . Many papers suffer because managements cannot make up their minds who they are aiming at. The result is often papers which lack identity and punch and therefore credibility, as nervous editors ignore the very stories they would major on if working for the local paper.*

Videos

Local authorities make limited use of videos, except on training courses. One example, however, is a county council which produced a video explaining the authority's aims, values and services, and made copies available on loan to all employees. In a similar way, some private sector companies use employee videos to supplement their annual reports.

It is a medium which would enable elected members and top management to be seen and heard by the whole workforce and so reduce the impersonality inherent in any large organisation. Its other advantage over the written word is that it can use powerful visual images to reinforce the message. For example, a video to explain the need for a shift from residential to community care in social services can show 'for real' what is involved in providing support for the elderly in their own homes. Pictures, in this type of context, speak very much louder than words.

Telephone and computer network messages

Another form of employee communication pioneered in the private sector is the use of recorded messages on the internal telephone system. For example, employees wanting information about the new pension regulations can dial an internal number and listen to a recorded explanation. For some staff, the spoken word is a more assimilable form of information than conventional written notices.

A similar principle, however, is used by a few local authorities within their computer network. In this case, the information is displayed on VDU screens. One large county council has a network of some 1,600 VDUs linking all its departments and major institutions and area offices. One of the facilities on this network is wide range of information about the county council (including all committee reports and minutes) which is openly available to all staff. The network can also be used to relay specific messages and to include interactive training programmes which staff can use individually as and when they have time.

Notice boards

Perhaps the most widely and unimaginatively used of all communication media is the staff notice board. Cluttered with a mixture of official and unofficial notices, pinned up in a haphazard fashion and often out-of-date, notice boards are often largely ignored by most employees. In this form they certainly cannot be relied on as a reliable means of getting information to all staff.

Their effectiveness can be markedly increased by more thought and effort being given to their siting, by providing different boards for official, unofficial and trade union notices, by frequent and regular weeding out of old notices, and by notices themselves being given graphic design treatment to ensure that they catch the eye—and are readable.

❑ Inter-management communication

It has been noted earlier in this chapter that the managerial role involves intensive interaction between managers. In this form of communication, too, there are numerous choices of communication mode. In particular:

■ Informal, face-to-face contact. For the confident manager, this is usually the most effective way of developing good working relationships and influencing other managers. Managers lacking in self-confidence often avoid this form of communication and use internal memos or convene formal meetings at which they can be supported by members of their staff. The chief executive of one authority felt it necessary to break the memo habit by formally banning it and insisting that all chief officers' contacts with him were to be by personal contact or telephone. While this may appear to be a somewhat extreme action, reluctance to rely on informal face-to-face contact does seem to be a significant symptom of organisational ossification in some parts of the public service.

■ Formal meetings. Part of the stereotype of the clumsy bureaucracy is a superfluity of formal meetings—particularly those in which no section or department is represented by a single manager. One authority, for example, was renowned for its managers attending meetings in threes. While formal meetings can obviously be over-used, they are a very effective means of communication when it is valuable to assemble an array of different professional or service talents to ensure that all relevant angles of an issue have been examined, and to stimulate the fresh thinking which can come from the interaction between different viewpoints.

- Memos, telephones, electronic mail. A manager needing to express a view to another manager, or to give or request information, has a choice between personal contact and these three less direct forms. Memos are useful when the message is either complex or needs to be recorded. The telephone will probably save time against a personal contact, and some managers find it a more effective medium than face-to-face discussion for getting quick answers from their colleagues. Electronic mail provides a new form of communication which in some managers' experience offers several advantages over conventional channels—provided that the messaging is direct and personal from one manager to another via their own desk-top terminals and not through the intermediary of secretaries. On this direct basis, it provides the confidentiality of face-to-face contact, avoids the time loss of lengthy telephone discussions, and solves the frustrating problem of being unable to make immediate contact because of engaged telephone lines or the manager being inaccessible at meetings. Managers who use their own terminals for electronic messaging soon develop a pithy, informal style of communication which is unique to this medium.

❑ Essential principles

In any discussion about communications, it is easy for interest in the technology of communicating to obscure the essential principles which should govern any authority's communications strategy. It needs to be recognised, too, that there is a need for a strategy. If the whole workforce is to be knowledgeable about, and supportive of, the authority's values and objectives, communication cannot be left to the initiative of individual managers. Some will communicate well, others poorly, and the information and messages so relayed will be lacking in consistency and coherence.

An Industrial Society pamphlet (*Understanding the Economic Facts*, Industrial Society, 1980) emphasises four key principles:

> ... *if facts are to be believed, and those who give them are to be trusted, the information must be: REGULAR, not just at a time of crisis or in the context of annual negotiations. HONEST, the facts both good and bad. OPEN to all employees, not just to management and union representatives, with a chance to ask questions. RELEVANT, primarily about the local unit for which employees work and whose performance they can directly affect.*

While these principles are put forward by the Industrial Society in relation only to the provision to employees of economic or financial information, the qualities of regularity, honesty, openness and relevance are applicable to all aspects of communication. Effective communication is the glue which holds together the otherwise separate and potentially conflicting parts of any organisation.

QUESTIONS ABOUT YOUR OWN AUTHORITY

- Is there a communication strategy?

- Are managers at all levels expected or required regularly to brief their employees?

- What formal and informal means exist for employees to relay their views to management or members?

- Are employee communications written in understandable language and presented in an attractive format?

- What communication modes are used (e.g. newsletters, notices, videos, briefing groups, consultative meetings, computer networks, etc.)?

- On what topics are employees given information on a regular basis (e.g. work achievements, service plans, budgets, etc.)?

8
Team and group working

KEY POINTS

- All jobs involve interaction with other jobs.

- Work groups or teams may be permanent or temporary, and set within departments or functions or be cross-functional.

- Chief officers' management teams work best when their function has been defined, their emphasis is on joint problem solving and they have a sense of common purpose.

- Cross-functional teams can co-ordinate activities which cross conventional departmental boundaries.

- The criteria for effective team working are:
  —a strong sense of team identity;
  —small scale: ideally, single-figure membership;
  —a sense of common purpose and a will to co-operate;
  —action or output orientation;
  —resources (information, specialist input, administration) and a mix of skills and style;
  —effective team leadership;
  —regular self-review of progress and performance.

- Teams can be helped to develop effectively by:
  —ensuring a mix of personalities;
  —providing them with assistance in examining their own group dynamics;
  —ensuring that the team activity is structured (e.g. agendas, deadlines, output targets, action notes, etc.).

No employee works in isolation. The amount of interaction with other employees varies considerably from job to job, but in all cases there are working links and communication upwards to senior staff and sideways to working colleagues. But these patterns of interaction go beyond merely linking each employee with a manager and with some other individual staff. There are clusters of links which represent groups of staff working closely together.

These groupings may be permanent—such as a chief officers' management group—or be formed for a fixed period to deal with a specific task—a working party or project team. They may also be part of the formal organisation structure—say, a departmental management team—or cross normal organisational boundaries.

Effective teams are more than just the sum of the efforts of their individual members: they produce ideas or other outputs which their members, working alone, would not achieve. Unfortunately, the reverse is also true: poorly functioning teams inhibit individual initiative and either fail to achieve any significant output or produce positively bad decisions. The development of team skills is consequently just as important as the development of the individual employee—though is often given much less managerial attention.

❏ Types of teams

Some forms of work require close, continuous team working. An example is a payroll section in which the work is planned as a flow process which requires each employee to match his or her work to that of the employees immediately behind and in front within the work flow. This type of team working is common in manufacturing industry, but less so in local authorities. Here, the most common form of team is one in which the team members have their own

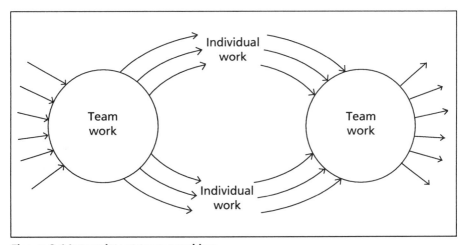

Figure 8.1 Intermittent team working

distinct and separate jobs, but come together from time to time to agree objectives, and allocate and co-ordinate individual tasks. Figure 8.1 illustrates this process: it is a form of team working which applies to both permanent and temporary teams.

Permanent teams

The permanent local government team with the highest profile is the chief officers' management group, chaired by the chief executive. There are exceedingly few authorities in which some or all chief officers do not meet regularly in this way to consider authority-wide issues and to keep each other informed of significant service matters. Their membership may vary from as few as three major directors to the heads of all departments which may number fifteen or more. Where the membership is large, some chief executives supplement the meetings with separate, usually less formal, and more frequent meetings with an 'inner cabinet' such as the director of operational services and central support services. Other heads of services sometimes view this practice with considerable suspicion, seeing it as a centralist and possibly secretive cabal.

There has been no extensive research on the effectiveness of chief officers' management groups (or directors' boards as they are sometimes termed) but anecdotal evidence and observation reveals a very wide range of practice and impact. Some examples illustrate good and bad features of these teams.

- In one authority, the chief officers' group is used by its members primarily to defend their own individual departmental interests—particularly in the annual budgetary competition for the biggest possible slice of a diminishing financial cake. Service departments, in particular, see the group as a mechanism for weakening the influence of central departments such as finance and personnel. While each service chief fights for his or her corner, all operational services band together in common cause against what they see as the dangers of centralism.

- At the other extreme, a neighbouring authority's management group provides each service with an annual opportunity to make a full presentation of its changing pressures and plans at which constructive comment by all the other chiefs is positively welcomed. The resulting service strategies carry the support of the whole group, and resource priorities—while still the subject of intense debate—are based on a common understanding of the important issues affecting each service.

In this group, too, the role of central departments as being primarily supportive of operational services is fully accepted, while the group as a whole discusses and agrees the issues on which authority-wide consistency is desirable.

■ In one borough, the director's board is perceived by elected members to be a powerful mechanism by which the top management plans its strategies to keep members at bay and to manipulate the bureaucratic machine for its own ends.

■ In another, members see the chief officers' group as being an essential and valuable part of the whole process of producing well-informed and constructive officer advice for members' benefit. In this authority, members often ask for matters to be considered by the whole chief officers' group before final committee decisions are reached, as they feel this ensures that a wider view will be reached than if advice emanates only from a single service chief.

■ One chief executive who considered himself a poor chairman—and who wished to be free to argue for a particular viewpoint without the constraints of being the group leader—arranged for each chief officer to chair the group meetings in turn. He considered that this not only freed him to participate more fully, but also helped in the personal development of the chief officers. The chief officers themselves had divided views about this, some looking to the chief executive for more positive direction, others welcoming the freedom of discussion which this approach encouraged.

There is little doubt that chief officers' groups which work well do so for three main reasons:

■ Their function has been clearly defined, and explained to and agreed with the elected members.

■ The emphases in their work are on joint problem solving, the identification of issues which require authority-wide action or consistency, and the co-ordination of officer advice to members in a way which supports and enhances the authority's strategic objectives.

■ They have a corporate sense of common purpose and are ably led.

Most chief officers who are members of a chief officers' group are also the leaders of their own departmental management teams—and members of these teams are also in turn the leaders of divisional or section teams. This

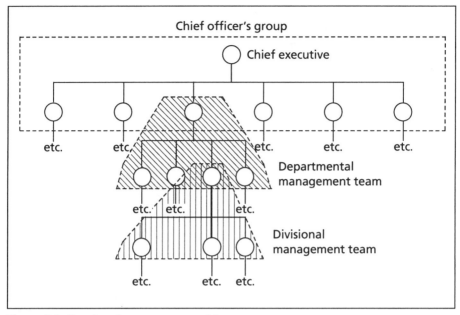

Figure 8.2 Overlapping management teams

pattern of overlapping membership is illustrated in Figure 8.2. This overlap indicates a need for team members to be able to cope with different roles in different teams. A team in which every member is hankering for the leadership position is unlikely to be any more effective than a football team full of sweepers.

Most chief officers hold regular meetings with the managers who report directly to them, and these departmental management teams fulfil the same functions within each service as the chief officers' group does for the authority as a whole. The finance department of one borough describes the main purposes of its management team as 'communication and co-ordination, and the formulation of departmental policy. It forms a readily convenient channel for information and the exchange of problems throughout the department: a forum where any matters of concern be they trivial or earth-shattering can be discussed openly and in confidence. At the same time, a corporate approach can be taken to problems internal and external to the department ... a mechanism for ensuring even and equitable treatment of staff ...'

In any large department, particularly one with a number of disparate divisional or area functions, one of the most important roles for management teams is to ensure that all the constituent parts of the department know what the others are doing, and to identify gaps or overlaps in these otherwise separate activities. The essence of team working is the development of shared information, understanding, objectives and commitment.

Some permanent teams cross the normal departmental boundaries and are used to co-ordinate activities which require on-going inter-departmental action. Thus, one county has established a permanent Landscape Working Party, consisting of third-tier officers from the planning, highways, architects', estates and education departments. The role of this body is to bring together all the main services which have an impact on landscape matters (either as major land users or as specialists) and to evolve landscape policies and programmes which are submitted to the chief officers' management group for endorsement. The working party has a small 'pump-priming' budget to spend on landscaping schemes which no one service would otherwise initiate.

Other examples of permanent inter-departmental teams include those concerned with such cross-departmental issues as the reduction of vandalism, the promotion of equal opportunities, and service provision for the parents and children of one-parent families. There are examples, too, of such working groups spanning both district and county councils—in the co-ordination, for example, of agency arrangements for highways maintenance and waste disposal. Successful teams of these kinds emphasise the importance of a very clear definition of their functions and of the limits to their decision-making powers. Experience also points to the need to review the purpose and performance of such teams from time to time, and to disband them if they outlive their usefulness.

Temporary teams

The use of a working group or working party to examine and report on a specific problem or to co-ordinate the implementation of a particular project, is widespread in local government. Such teams may be within a department— and then monitored by the departmental management team—or inter-departmental. Their proliferation sometimes leads towards a cynical view that 'when in doubt, form a working party', and from observation it is clear that the value of such teams varies from the highly productive to the wholly ineffective. A few examples illustrate this.

- One authority set up a working party of all 14 of its deputy chief officers to produce a management development strategy. Not all the team were particularly enthusiastic about the task and attendance at their meetings was very variable. There was a reluctance to take the chair— no one had been nominated to take on this role—and by default the chair was eventually taken by a deputy who was within a few months of an early retirement. No arrangements were made to provide any specialist or administrative support. After six months it became evident that the team were making little progress and the working party was disbanded. It was replaced by a smaller group of second- and third-tier managers who were enthusiasts for the subject, led by a nominated officer with a reputation for effective team leadership and 'getting things done', and aided by high-level external specialist advice and internal professional support. This team quickly developed a strong sense of ownership of the issue and a commitment to action.

- Another authority established a working party to review the possible decentralisation of the finance function. There had been an impasse on the subject in the chief officers' management group and the idea of a working party of third-tier officers had been suggested by the chief executive as a way of defusing the arguments. The working party consisted of three central finance staff who were as opposed to decentralisation as their director, and three service managers who strongly supported the concept. It soon became evident that it was as impossible for this team to reach agreement as it had been for the chief officers' group. The matter was eventually resolved by the chief executive setting up a three-person review team of senior corporate staff with no personal finance or service interests whose proposals were accepted as impartial.

- A district council became very concerned about its generally poor public image. With the backing of the elected members, the chief officers' group commissioned a study of the problem by an external consultant, but set up a working group of two chief officers, two deputies and two third-tier managers—all of whom had expressed great interest in the issue from several different viewpoints—to work with the consultant. The outcome initially was a report setting out an action programme which was enthusiastically endorsed by the council, and at that point the consultant left the scene. The officers' working party was kept in existence for the next 12 months to oversee the very successful implementation of a wide range of measures which improved dramatically the council's public standing and reputation.

These examples of successful and unsuccessful teams lead into an examination of the criteria for effective team working.

❑ Effective team working

Whether temporary or permanent, teams which work well have a number of common characteristics. Effective team working may occur accidentally, but the chances of failure are far too high to leave success to chance. An understanding of the criteria for success is an essential element of effective human resource management in a team context. One authority, which placed great importance on the development of teams, listed the criteria for success as:

- Team members must see themselves as a team—there must be a strong sense of, and pride in, team identity.

- Good teams are usually small teams—numbers are best kept in single figures.

- There must be a common goal or goals—team members must have a sense of common purpose.

- There must be a will to co-operate.

- A team needs a mix of skills, experience, knowledge and personality.

From other sources, four other factors can be suggested which contribute to team success:

- Teams should be action- or output-oriented. Meetings held merely for discussion purposes can waste time and effort. Teams need to have set, or set for themselves, an agenda for action, with deadlines.

- Teams usually need resources; they are rarely self-sufficient. This may involve the co-option of specialists to provide an input of knowledge. In almost all cases, there is a need for administrative support.

- Effective team leadership is a must: teams cannot operate as undirected or uninspired collectives.

- Teams need to keep their own performance under review, and to take stock from time to time about how well they are operating and the extent to which they are achieving more than their members could do acting individually.

Most of these points are illustrated by the examples of good and poor team working quoted earlier.

- The weak management development team had too many members—it is all but impossible to form an effective working group with as many as 14 participants. The team members had inadequate commitment; there was inadequate leadership and no resource support. The replacement team corrected all these flaws—it was smaller (nine members), all were enthusiastic about their task, they were well led, and adequate specialist and administrative support was made available.

- The team reviewing decentralisation failed initially because it was set up on the basis of conflict, not co-operation. Its members saw their roles as to protect their separate interests, not to promote the authority's corporate interest. The successful team took the latter view.

- The successful public-image team met all the criteria listed above. They were a small group who quickly developed a strong sense of identity and common purpose. They had a will to co-operate in order to achieve an important result. They constituted a good mix of skills, experience and personality. They had adequate resources. They worked to an action plan and frequently reviewed their own progress.

❏ Team development

Positive action to improve team performance can be seen as part of a spectrum of development which ranges from the training of managers as individuals, at one extreme, to the overall development of the whole authority (organisational development), at the other. Figure 8.3 illustrates this.

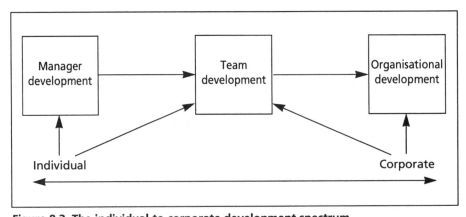

Figure 8.3 The individual to corporate development spectrum

Three main elements are involved:

- selection of team members;

- developing team understanding;

- structuring the team process.

Selecting team members

It has already been suggested that a team comprised solely of budding leaders is heading for trouble. No team can operate effectively if rivalry for dominance is a major motivator for most of its members. Ideally, a mix of personality types is needed to bring a range of perceptions and approaches to the team process. Of particular value are the following roles:

- A leader who can stimulate free-flowing debate without dominating the discussion, but who can also keep sufficient control to ensure that the right balance is struck between the important and the peripheral; and that outcomes are positive and within time constraints.

- An analytical member, who helps the team to separate out the constituent parts of a complex issue, without necessarily expressing a strong personal view about solutions.

- A pragmatist, who brings the team down to earth from time to time by reminding them of hard reality and who asks 'who is going to do what, and by when?'

- A lateral thinker who can suggest new and unconventional directions.

- An idealist who can bring a touch of inspiration to counter cynicism or pessimism.

- A conciliator, often with a well-rounded sense of humour, who can restore good relations if negative conflict begins to develop.

A mix of knowledge, skills and experience is also valuable, as too narrow a range of specialism—however expert—can lead to unrealistic outcomes. The experience of two authorities' working groups on competitive tendering can be contrasted:

- The first set up a team consisting of one senior line manager from each of the four operational service departments most directly affected, plus one officer each from the finance, personnel, legal and supplies departments. They produced a set of organisational and procedural strategies which the authority feels will provide an excellent basis for achieving its value-for-money policy. The wide mix of skills and perceptions ensured that all possible angles were explored and a balance of interests achieved.

■ The other authority also established an inter-departmental working party, but limited its membership to the finance, management services and legal departments. They produced plans which the service chief officers rejected as damagingly unrealistic because they failed to reflect service realities.

The importance of the right mix of personalities and experience points to a problem with permanent teams such as chief officers' groups and departmental management teams. Here, officers are in these teams because they have been selected for their ability to head departments or sections, not for their team membership qualities. In that they all have to lead their own groups, they may well all tend towards the assertive, executive role. Clearly they cannot be selected on the basis of ensuring a good mix of personalities, but this factor may nevertheless need to be borne in mind as one (though not the dominant) of the factors in their selection.

The situation is easier when temporary groups are being put together. Here, there is usually a degree of choice and more attention can be given to obtaining a wide range of personalities. Some authorities use personality tests to help in this process.

Developing team understanding

Effective team working may just happen as the chance result of an ideal blend of experience and personality. Too often, though, the high level of performance which a good team can reach is never achieved—often because the team has never actively considered its own performance or analysed the reasons why it is working poorly.

At the heart of effective team working is the quality of personal relationships between the team's members. Teams cannot operate well if these relationships are marked by mistrust, rivalry for dominance and reticence in expressing different viewpoints. The essence of good team working is openness in discussion, with everyone feeling free to contribute and all willing to listen to the other person's point of view. Good teams are not afraid of conflict: they understand the value of every new idea being tested by opposing arguments. They use conflict constructively to generate ideas and solutions which can withstand the most critical scrutiny.

Describing good team working is much easier than achieving it, and many teams have found external help of great value in improving their collective performance. Team training is consequently being used to an increasing extent by many authorities. This normally involves a training officer or consultant working with the team, helping them to understand the dynamics of the team process. An example can be drawn from one authority's planning department whose newly appointed chief officer restructured the department, acquired a team of six senior planning managers who had not previously worked together, and found initially that at team meetings most of these managers contributed only to defend their own specialist interests. He sought assistance from the training manager who then worked with the team over a six-month period. Team development activities included:

- A residential weekend at a remote country hotel at which departmental policies and objectives were considered.

- Some formal training input about the nature of team dynamics.

- The completion of personality profiles by the team members and a discussion of the implications for the team of the particular mix of personalities which the profiles revealed.

- Several open-ended (and initially painful) discussions in which the training manager acted as a catalyst in stimulating an examination of the blockages to good team working which were being experienced.

- Several team-building exercises to illustrate the need for team objectives, mutual support, openness and trust if the objectives were to be met.

Not all teams require the comprehensive approach of this example. Some may already have built up the necessary internal trust and confidence, but may lack positive direction. Others may have an excellent blend of skills and a sense of purpose, but have not yet been bonded into a corporate unit. A starting point for team development is therefore often a discussion—aided by an outside facilitator who can 'innocently' ask awkward questions—about how the team is performing and what assistance it needs if it is to do better. Team development is essentially self-development; it cannot be imposed on a team unwilling to admit that it needs help.

Structuring the team process

Although the dynamics of team working are of vital importance, teams should not become so fascinated by the inter-play of their own internal relationships that they forget that their purpose is functional—the production of action plans, policies or solutions. The point is illustrated by one powerful form of team training—outdoor activity work in which, for example, a team may be set the task of crossing a river within a set time, given only a few planks, an oil drum and some rope. How well the team works is tested ultimately not by an abstract discussion of team dynamics, but by whether the team crosses the river.

In the management context, teams need to operate within at least a framework of procedure. Five particular points can be used as a checklist:

- Is an agenda and any necessary data or discussion paper issued in sufficient time for the team members individually to digest and consider the issues to be discussed?

- Does the team leader start by ensuring an understanding of what the meeting is designed to achieve?

- Does the team allocate its time effectively, giving priority to the most important items? (One chief officer always takes 'matters arising' last instead of first in order to avoid the bad use of time spent in going over old ground.)

- At the end of the meeting, does the leader summarise the position which has been reached and ensure that any agreed action has been clearly allocated and new deadlines set?

- Does the team take time out from time to time (perhaps twice a year) to review its own collective behaviour and performance?

These points can be applied to permanent teams, such as chief officers' groups, and to time-limited inter-departmental working parties. For the latter, however, there is one additional factor. This is the link between the working party, which is not part of the permanent organisational hierarchy, and the formal and permanent structure of decision-making and authority. The reporting relationships for working parties are sometimes rather vague—is it to a nominated chief officer, to the chief executive, to the corporate management team or even direct to a committee? And, if the latter, is it free to put forward views which may not have been discussed or agreed within the top management hierarchy?

It is often helpful, too, for the leader of a working party to have access, on a counselling or mentoring basis, to a senior manager who is not part of the team. Working outside the formal structures can be a difficult and lonely role, and advice on how to proceed can be extremely helpful to the team leader who becomes aware of this.

QUESTIONS ABOUT YOUR OWN AUTHORITY

- Is the role of the chief officers' group clearly understood by its members, by other managers, by councillors?

- Is it seen as contributing positively to the achievement of the authority's objectives?

- Do all departments make effective use of management teams?

- How are inter-departmental issues or services dealt with? Are there any standing inter-departmental working groups? If so, is their role clearly defined, and do they have the authority and resources to be effective?

- When selecting members of working groups, is consideration given to the need for a blend of skills and personalities?

- Is any team training or development provided?

9

Equal opportunities

KEY POINTS

- Action to promote equality of opportunity is required by law, reduces social divisiveness, and equates to good employment practice.

- At its simplest, equal opportunity means 'don't generalise'.

- The criteria for an effective equal opportunity programme are:
  —producing and publicising an equal opportunity policy;
  —allocating responsibility for achieving the policy to an appropriate committee, and to all managers;
  —providing a functional focus, usually the chief personnel officer;
  —reviewing and revising all employment procedures;
  —training managers in non-discriminatory practices;
  —communicating with all sections of the community;
  —consulting with employees and their trade unions;
  —monitoring the implementation of the policy.

Securing genuine equality of opportunity needs to be seen as an integral element of human resource management, not as some form of optional extra. The essence of the human resource concept is that every individual has a greater capacity for achievement than traditional systems of management recognise, and that there is consequently an untapped reservoir of human skill and endeavour which a more imaginative and holistic approach should release. It makes no sense, therefore, for all but the least skilled sectors of employment to continue to be staffed predominantly by that part of the population which is male, white, able-bodied and, at management level, middle-aged. This restricts employee talent, shutting out the wider range of experience and skill which a more broadly drawn workforce would provide.

There are three other levels of justification for taking equal opportunities seriously:

- The law prohibits discrimination based on race, sex or marital status; and requires a positive approach to the employment of people with disabilities.

- Equal opportunity action equates to good general employment practice.

- Prejudice and discrimination are socially divisive and morally indefensible.

On all three counts, responsible public employers such as local authorities ought surely to take a lead, though compliance with the law may be taken as an obvious starting point.

❏ What the law requires

In the fields of race, sex and marital status, the main statutes (Race Relations 1976 and Sex Discrimination Acts 1975 and 1986) bar direct and indirect discrimination. Indirect discrimination occurs when the effect of an employment practice is to the disadvantage of women or particular ethnic groups, even though that effect is not intended. For example, one authority's career structure used to include two quite separate streams—clerical and administrative. Promotions from the clerical to the administrative stream were very rare, not least because the age and qualification criteria for administrative trainees were biased strongly towards graduates in their early twenties. Older clerical staff could sometimes demonstrate obvious ability to progress into administrative work, but were prevented by the selection criteria. The system worked unwittingly to the disadvantage of women, who formed the vast majority of the clerical grades. This unintended indirect discrimination ended when a unified career structure was introduced spanning all clerical and administrative work, and when the rigid age criteria were abandoned.

The legislation is supported by Codes of Practice issued by the two statutory bodies responsible for promoting equality of opportunity—the Commission for Racial Equality and the Equal Opportunity Commission. The Codes have a similar legal standing to the Highway Code: they are not directly enforceable at law, but compliance or otherwise is taken into account by industrial tribunals or the courts in assessing whether an employer has taken adequate steps to comply with the statutes.

The Acts and Codes permit and encourage positive action in the field of training (i.e. training specifically for women or black people) where a particular group is significantly under-represented in the workforce. Positive action is barred, however, in the selection of individual candidates for jobs, except in very limited circumstances which are defined in the statutes. (Expert legal and personnel advice is recommended before making use of this exception—known as 'genuine occupational qualifications'.)

The Race Relations Act lays an additional statutory duty on local authorities—to promote non-discriminatory practice in all aspects of service delivery, as well as in employment.

The Equal Pay Act requires not just the same pay for men and women doing the same work, but equal pay for work or equal value. Value in this respect requires comparative assessments to be made of the levels of skill, effort and responsibility involved in specified jobs done by women and men respectively.

The law treats disability differently from race and sex. There is no statutory bar on discrimination against the disabled. Instead, employers are required to employ 3% of registered disabled persons—or if that proves impracticable, obtain a formal waiver. In early 1995, the Government produced proposals for major changes, including the abolition of the quota but stronger legislative measures to inhibit discrimination and improve access to buildings and services.

❏ Good employment practice

Although the statutes provide a base-line for action, they do not cover some common forms of prejudice and discrimination—such as rigid age limits— and have not proved sufficient to do much more than prevent gross and overt discrimination.

A growing number of employers in the private as well as public sector have consequently overhauled all their employment procedures to achieve non-discriminatory practice as a matter of sound, general employment policy. Commercial organisations have taken such action partly because of a sense of social responsibility. In the main, however, their motivation has been commercial good sense: they consider that a socially well-balanced workforce is a better workforce. The company's effectiveness is improved and its reputation as an employer is enhanced.

In local government, equal opportunity action has sometimes been perceived as political symbolism. This has had the unfortunate effect of generating adverse political reaction—an avoidance of a commitment to equal opportunities because such action is seen as politically biased. Fortunately, this attitude is far less common in the mid 1990s than it was a decade earlier.

A wider argument for action

There is another argument and it is essentially simple and humanistic. It is based on the fact that almost all employment action comes down eventually to decisions about individuals—who to select for a particular job, who to promote or send on a training course, who to be selected for redundancy, and so on. When these decisions are being made, every individual has the right to be assessed for his or her own personal qualities, and not against any generalised assumptions. The underlying message in all equal opportunity action is *don't generalise!* And this goes well beyond the categories of discrimination covered by statute.

Discrimination is characterised by the application of generalities to individuals. 'West Indians are carefree.' 'Women cannot make tough decisions.' 'Too old at 50.' 'Unmarried men over 30 are probably gay.' Generalised assumptions of these kinds are rife and influence far too many employment decisions. Individuals are assessed quickly and casually against these stereotypes rather than against carefully thought-out criteria and a proper assessment of each person's individual qualities. Decisions made in this way are sheer bad employment practice: they also demean the individual and reinforce unhealthy social divisions.

The general character of an approach to equal opportunities based on compliance with the law, good employment practice and the wider moral or social view can be illustrated by the following extract from a *Handbook of Good Employment Practice* issued by one large local authority to all its managers and supervisors:

> ... *The achievement of an equal opportunity policy is not primarily dependent on special or unusual measures, but rather on fair and effective employment practices across the whole range of employment decisions, whether or not such decisions are subject to specific legislation ...*
>
> *Unfair and poor quality employment decisions can result from generalised assumptions being made on many bases such as age, domestic circumstances, accent, colour, sexual orientation, religion or disability. The Council's policy and this Handbook are concerned with ensuring that no individuals or groups are disadvantaged by such common prejudices as 'too old at 50' or 'this is a job for a man', whether or not such discrimination is unlawful.*

> *This is a positive, not negative approach. Employees will benefit from the greater attention paid to their personal and career development. By concentrating on the positive requirements of jobs, and on the unique aptitudes and abilities of people as individuals, the Council will also be able to draw on the widest possible range of talents in the delivery and management of its services.*

❑ Putting an equal opportunity policy into effect

There is a great deal more to equal opportunity action than using the slogan 'An Equal Opportunity Employer' in job advertisements. Indeed, if action is limited to sloganising, with no real changes in employment practice, the result will be worse than taking no action at all.

A report produced by the Association of County Councils suggests that ten elements are involved in producing a comprehensive and effective action programme:

- A formal policy statement is adopted to demonstrate the authority's commitment.

- The policy is publicised internally and externally.

- Responsibility for the evolution and oversight of the policy at elected member level is allocated to an appropriate committee.

- Management staff, from the chief executive down, are seen to be responsible for ensuring the policy's practical application.

- Functional responsibility for evolving, advising on and monitoring the necessary action is allocated to an appropriate senior or chief officer, usually the chief personnel officer, who is also allocated some additional resources to assist in implementation.

- Employment procedures are reviewed, revised and extended to incorporate the necessary equal opportunity elements.

- Training is provided to ensure that managers have the necessary understanding and skills to implement revised employment practices.

- Staff and trade-union consultation and information is effected in order to secure employee understanding and commitment.

- The policy is communicated carefully to the whole community, both the indigenous majority and the disadvantaged groups.

■ The implementation and results of the policy are kept under systematic review, with progress reports being made to the relevant committee.

Three aspects of equal opportunity action are the subject of considerable debate and disagreement—sometimes to the point of inhibiting action on less contentious aspects. These issues are monitoring, positive action and targeting.

Monitoring

It is an accepted general managerial principle that all policies require a feedback system to ensure their effectiveness. Figure 9.1 illustrates this. Thus if one objective of an equal opportunity policy is to increase the proportion of women in managerial jobs, this loop process requires that the actual numbers are monitored, so that the effectiveness of the policy can be checked and, if necessary, improved. No difficulties occur in monitoring employment decisions involving women or the registered disabled, as personnel records always hold data on gender and registered disability. It has not been as common to keep records of candidates' or employees' ethnic origin. Yet to assess the effectiveness of equal opportunity policies in the field of race, information about the numbers of people from minority groups applying and appointed to jobs, or trained and promoted, is obviously necessary.

The Commission for Racial Equality, supported by other bodies such as the Institute of Personnel and Development, recommends that such records be kept; and a growing number of well-known companies—as well as the Civil Service and many local authorities—have introduced ethnic records of job applicants and employees.

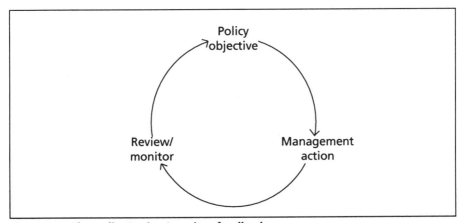

Figure 9.1 The policy/action/monitor feedback process

The introduction of ethnic records needs to be handled sensitively if adverse employee reaction is to be avoided. Suddenly to send forms to employees without prior explanation, seeking self-classification of their ethnic origins will probably result in confusion and suspicion, and will certainly not achieve a 100% response rate. When one county council first issued a questionnaire to its employees in this way (seeking self-classification as Asian, Afro-Caribbean, UK/Eire, Other European and Other) the response rate was only about 40%. Only after a second campaign in which considerable effort was put into explaining the reasons to employees and providing guarantees of confidentiality was the response rate raised to nearer 90%.

The experience of this county, and of many other public- and private-sector employers, points to monitoring undertaken by managers as the most successful method. Managers can explain the reasons for monitoring to their staff, deal personally with some employees' initial fears or objections, and then complete a simple return, classifying their staff within a simple categorisation such as that in the county example above.

Positive action

There is often confusion about the difference between positive action, which is lawful, and positive discrimination which, with very few exceptions, is unlawful.

Positive action is based on the principle that it is good practice, to quote one authority's equal opportunity policy, 'to take such action as is necessary to disadvantaged groups reach a position from which genuine equality of opportunity can operate'. Two examples of such action follow:

■ Several authorities run managerial or career development training courses specifically for women staff. The LGMB launched a national Women's Programme in 1994, designed to assist more women reach senior managerial positions. Women are significantly under-represented in managerial posts, and the Sex Discrimination Act permits single-sex training courses for work in which such under-representation occurs. This does not imply favouring individual women above men when appointments are made—that would be unlawful positive discrimination. The purpose of these courses is to provide women collectively with the knowledge and confidence needed for individuals to compete on level terms with men.

■ In the field of disability, several authorities operate schemes under which disabled people are recruited initially into a central pool. Here they are provided with training, planned work experience and, if necessary, physical aids to equip them to compete for normal jobs on level terms with the able-bodied.

Positive discrimination means appointing a person solely or mainly because of their race or gender. It is almost wholly barred by law, the only exceptions being when there is what the statutes describe as a 'genuine occupational qualification'. Examples include the recruitment of a black social worker in a post established specifically to assist a local black community; or where, in a residential establishment, it is impracticable to provide separate sanitary or sleeping arrangements for male and female staff and, in consequence, staff of only one sex can be employed.

Targets

A more controversial development, adopted by only a few authorities, is the setting of statistical targets for the number or proportion of women or black people to be employed. The principle is a simple one, based on good general management practice—that of setting objectives.

If the purpose of an equal opportunity policy is to achieve a more balanced workforce, it seems sensible to have some idea as to what this means: 50% of managerial jobs held by women? 5% of all jobs held by black people because they constitute 5% of the local population? Proponents of targets say that well-meaning but vague phrases about the elimination of discrimination lack the definition needed to ensure that progress is made. So targeting is the setting of goals for achievement.

Targets should not be confused with quotas. Quotas—in the sense of numbers or proportions which have to be met regardless of any other considerations— require the type of positive discrimination which is wholly unlawful. Targets are something to work towards over time and against which trends and progress can be assessed. They are objectives which may well require revision in the light of experience. A parallel might be the setting of a target profit ratio of 10% for a highways DSO. This does not imply that the 10% is mandatory— it is the objective by which the standard of performance of the DSO is assessed.

Nevertheless, because of the acute sensitivities involved in equal opportunity action, any authority introducing the target concept will need to do a great deal of preliminary explanation, internally and publicly. Without such preparation, assumptions or allegations will certainly be made that targets = quotas = discriminating in favour of certain groups.

❏ Basic action

Disagreement or delay in pursuing monitoring, positive action or targeting need not prevent much useful and more basic action being implemented to combat prejudice and discrimination. The following checklist illustrates the range of such action which many authorities have found practicable and constructive.

■ In job specifications, discard any criteria other than those which are demonstrably essential.

■ Stop word-of-mouth recruitment: it perpetuates the existing composition of the workforce. Use a wide range of recruitment media.

■ Do not use application forms as a test of literacy for jobs in which literacy is not a significant job requirement.

■ Ensure that all staff involved in selection interviewing are given adequate training which includes an equal opportunity component.

■ Support an equal opportunity policy by training programmes, particularly for managers, in its underlying principles (sometimes termed awareness training) and in the legislative background.

■ Examine how employees are recruited, selected and promoted, and eliminate any direct or indirect bias which may be inherent in existing procedures and criteria.

■ Ensure that adequate procedures exist to deal with sexual or racial harassment, and that all employees realise that such harassment is a disciplinary offence.

■ Examine all conditions of service for direct or indirect bias, paying particular attention to job grading (i.e. the need for equal pay for equal value), arrangements to assist employees with career breaks for domestic reasons, and the granting of compassionate leave.

■ Involve trade unions, and members of potentially disadvantaged groups such as the disabled, in consultations about employment policies and procedures.

■ Ensure that all employees understand the policy and the positive part they, as well as managers, need to play in the acceptance and integration of colleagues from other than conventional backgrounds.

The long-term aim should be to build equal opportunity thinking and action into all employment practices, not to establish on any permanent basis a special set of procedures. There is an analogy with safety policies and measures. Good working practices are safe working practices. Safety is not something special which can be added to 'normal' working procedures. It is something all managers should accept responsibility for and integrate with normal work design and operation. Similarly, good employment practice is bias-free employment practice— something which can be achieved only if all managers accept responsibility for such achievement as integral to their overall responsibilities for the effective management of the human resource.

QUESTIONS ABOUT YOUR OWN AUTHORITY

- Is there a formal policy? Has it been widely publicised and explained both to the workforce and the community?
- Which committee has responsibility for the policy?
- Do managers understand that it is their responsibility (not just that of any specialist staff) to put the policy into effect?
- Have managers been trained, e.g. in bias-free interviewing?
- Have all employment procedures been reviewed to eliminate bias?
- Has word-of-mouth recruitment been stopped?
- Do effective procedures exist to deal with sexual and racial harassment?
- Are there adequate consultative arrangements with trade unions and community groups?
- Do adequate review and monitoring procedures exist to show how well the policy is being implemented?

10

Industrial relations

- Trade unions provide an institutional, collective voice for employees, in which the ultimate authority lies with the membership.

- The conduct of industrial relations is strongly proceduralised and relies heavily on collective agreements and on precedent.

- Managers need to distinguish between consultation (joint discussion) and negotiation (joint agreement).

- The five broad levels of industrial relations in local government:
  —national: the national joint negotiating bodies;
  —regional: the Provincial Councils;
  —authority: council-wide consultation or negotiation;
  —departmental: relations within a single service;
  —workplace: the shop steward/manager relationship.

- The pressures on national bargaining:
  —more sharply defined and differing political principles between authorities;
  —competitive tendering and market forces;
  —concern about the divisiveness of the multiplicity of different employee categories.

- Managers need to develop negotiating skills—integrity, consistency, constructive determination, emotional control, analytical ability, effective communication and skills of interaction.

The management of people either as individual employees or as working groups is not the whole task of human resource management in local government. Trade unions play an important part in employer/employee relations. If an organisation such as a company or a local authority is viewed as a power structure, then trade unions can be seen as institutions which exist to give employees a countervailing influence to the otherwise dominating authority of management. Legally, the relationship between employer and employee is based on the concept of a contract in which each are equal partners. The reality, of course, is that this relationship is very unequal, with the power of the individual employee to influence or change the actions of the employer being miniscule in relation to the power of the organisation as a corporate body to override, if it so chooses, the interests of the single employee. Trade unions, therefore, came into existence (and largely remain) as institutions to give employees collectively an influence on the employer/employee relationship which is quite beyond the reach of the individual employee and which goes some way to restoring the power balance between them. This collective and institutionalised relationship has to be managed effectively if it is not to become negative or confrontational.

To do so requires from the manager in the first instance an acceptance of the reality of the existence of trade unions throughout the whole local government workforce. Problems in the management of industrial relations sometimes derive from an underlying resentment—conscious or unconscious—that within the workplace there is an institution which can challenge the authority, not just of the individual manager, but of the organisation as a whole. To the manager whose underlying concept of the management role is that of the autocrat (however benevolent), the ability of a trade union to challenge managerial decisions and in the ultimate to prevent their implementation by industrial action is understandably galling. But if a manager chooses to work in a unionised environment, coming to terms with this reality is a prerequisite to effective human resource management.

❏ General principles

Before examining the pattern of industrial relations at national, provincial and local levels, four further general points need to be considered:

- the nature of trade unions as institutions;
- the emphasis on protocol and procedures;
- the importance of precedent;
- consultation and negotiation.

Trade unions

In their relationships with trade unions, managers need to understand that a trade union differs fundamentally from a local authority in its system of internal power and authority. In employer organisations (companies, councils, etc.), power and authority flow from the top down. Boards of directors, or elected members in committee or council, determine policy and appoint managers to put policies into effect. Within this management hierarchy, authority starts at the top, with chief executives and chief officers, who may delegate part of their authority to subordinate managers.

In principle, this is wholly reversed in trade unions. Ultimate power and authority rest with the union membership at large, not with union presidents or general secretaries. There is no trade union in which the general membership could not, using the union's constitutional processes, ultimately alter or overturn the actions or appointment of its elected or appointed leaders—be these at national, regional or local level. The practice of employers' pay offers being submitted by the unions to their members for approval (by voting or through branch meetings) is a practical demonstration of this principle.

This major difference between trade unions and employers can cause difficulties and frustration for managers if it is not recognised. Figure 10.1 illustrates the position. The diagram shows power—and therefore decision-making—concentrated at the top in a local authority and at the bottom in a trade union. The middle manager, negotiating with a union branch, may therefore need to refer up the management line for approval to offer a

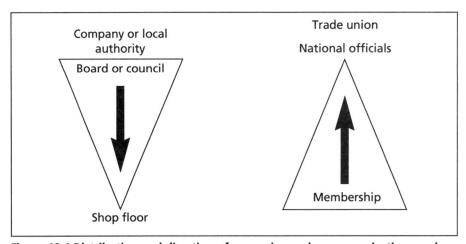

Figure 10.1 Distribution and direction of power in employer organisations and trade unions

particular concession. The union branch secretary may have to put the same point, not up to the regional secretary who the manager may assume is the branch secretary's boss, but down to the branch membership. Without an understanding of these power differences, manager and branch secretary may criticise each other for weakness. The manager may say: 'What's the point of trying to do a deal with you when you won't take the responsibility of making a decision?' To which the branch secretary may reply: 'Why should we waste time talking to you when you have to run back to your boss?

Procedures

The processes in industrial relations are strongly proceduralised or codified. This is not a bureaucratic trait specific to the public sector—it is a marked feature of the industrial relations scene throughout the whole economy. Trade unions and employers have found it helpful and indeed necessary to commit to paper the various agreements they reach, and to establish agreed patterns of interaction. Without such formality, experience on both sides is that disagreements will occur about respective rights and obligations, the same type of issue will have to be discussed time and time again, and mistrust will develop as each side suspects the other of trying to achieve a gradual erosion of the other's position. The main areas of codification are:

- Recognition agreements: for many categories of employees, there are potentially several different trade unions. It is important, therefore, to establish which trade unions the employer will do business with. In the white-collar sector, for example, should a local authority recognise MSF? Recognition agreements eliminate any confusion about this by specifying which unions are accepted by the employer (and by the union world) as representing which categories of employees. The general rule in local government is that the recognised unions are only those which are party to the various national agreements. On that basis, MSF would not be recognised as it is not in membership of the relevant National Joint Council.

- Facilities agreements: a potent cause of dispute between managers and trade unions is imprecision about such matters as the amount of time off shop stewards may have to attend union meetings, how many shop stewards or workplace representatives there should be (and who they are), and whether they may use the authority's notice boards or internal mail system. Facilities agreements specify all such issues.

- Consultation procedures: an important part of the working relationship between an authority and the trade unions is the consultation and discussion of matters of joint interest and concern. How frequently should such meetings occur? Who should attend? Are minutes to be kept? If so, who will produce them? Consultation procedures will specify an agreed format for joint consultative committees and processes.

- Disputes procedures: it would be unrealistic to expect the trade union/employer relationship always to be harmonious. Situations will sometimes arise in which the wish or action of the authority or the trade union is perceived by the other party as detrimental to its interest. How should such a difference be resolved? Contrary to the popular stereotype of the disruptive shop steward, unions are just as keen to resolve disputes quickly, effectively and without industrial action as are employers. Both sides have found by experience that the existence of an agreed procedural framework for handling disputes enables everyone to concentrate on finding solutions to problems, rather than wasting time and energy arguing about how to proceed. The inclusion of time-scales for moving a dispute up the hierarchy (local manager to divisional manager to chief officer to chief executive to elected members) also provides the union with protection against employer prevarication, and the authority with a discipline to produce results.

- Disciplinary procedures: the disciplining and possible dismissal of an employee is a stark example of the ultimate power of an employing organisation over an individual member of the workforce. One of the main protections which a trade union can offer its members is representation and defence when disciplinary action is being taken. There are legal as well as industrial relations reasons why formal procedures are desirable, but in a unionised situation it is normal for disciplinary procedures to be seen as part of the set of procedures which employer and trade unions are committed to follow.

- Grievance procedures: a very similar position exists for general employee grievances. How should the employee with a grievance raise the matter? Can he or she be assisted by a trade union? How should unresolved grievances at one level be raised with the next? Within what time-scales? Agreed procedures provide a mechanism for dealing with grievances on a consistent basis and prevent any ambiguity or disagreement about the role and rights of trade unions in their job of assisting the individual employee.

- Pay and conditions agreements: the largest area for the written specification of negotiated employee rights is, of course, the whole complex field of pay and other conditions of service. There is very obvious joint advantage to employer and trade union in setting down on paper precisely what has been agreed when so many matters—pay, leave, hours of work, allowances, overtime and so on—are subject to collective bargaining. Without such codification, arguments arise not just as to what a particular condition of service should be, but as to whether or not the matter has been the subject of discussion and, if so, what was agreed. If any difference of approach exists about this, it is that managers lean towards leaving at least some issues open to personal discretion, whereas trade unions prefer the maximum of detailed specification.

The main lesson for managers is—know your agreements and procedures. It is not uncommon for a manager to make an apparently wholly reasonable decision—say, about dealing informally with a complaint by an employee about the allocation of overtime—only to be faulted by the trade union for being in breach of agreed grievance procedures and of the national agreement about overtime. These breaches of procedures then become as much a matter of dispute as the original complaint. Personnel officers should be expertly knowledgeable about all these procedures and agreements. One of their roles is to advise managers accordingly—but they can often help only if the manager seeks their advice before taking action.

Precedents

Custom, practice and precedent are almost as powerful an influence on the conduct of industrial relations as formal procedures. In the absence of documented agreements or procedures, managers and trade unions refer back to established practices and previous decisions, and often treat these as having created a pattern of rights. Thus a trade union may object to disciplinary action for making private telephone calls from the office on the grounds that this practice has been going on for years and no one has ever been disciplined for it before. The management may try to counter this by producing evidence of a disciplinary hearing for this offence which took place several years before.

It is noteworthy that arguments of this kind about past practice often occupy as much or more time and energy as discussions about the specific issues of the case. The standard trade union view is that if something has been done in a particular way in the past, then any change must be a subject for negotiation. The management position is often that if some evidence can be produced to show that a decision is not entirely without precedent, then no negotiation is necessary.

Without attempting to abandon the whole principle of rights being established by precedent, the effective manager will nevertheless often wish to re-examine old customs in the light of changed current circumstances, and will consequently work towards interesting the trade unions in setting custom and practice on one side and redefining the issues.

Consultation and negotiation

The words 'consultation' and negotiation' have already been used in this chapter. They require definition as they are by no means synonymous:

- Negotiation implies acceptance by both employer and trade union that they need to agree about an issue before action is implemented.

- Consultation implies acceptance of the need for joint discussion, but reserves to the employer the ultimate and unilateral right of decision and implementation.

At the extremes, there is little difficulty in drawing the distinction. For example, many authorities have established a formal process for consulting the trade unions about the annual budget. Budget proposals are explained, and the unions are invited to express their views. The authority may, indeed, alter some of its budget plans to take account of the views so expressed. But at the end of the day, the final decision about the annual budget will be taken by members in full council. There is no question of concluding an agreement with the unions before this decision can be reached. The subject is one for consultation, not negotiation.

Similarly, it is generally accepted that changes to such conditions of service as basic pay rates or the standard working week are matters for negotiation, not just consultation. Changes are not made until agreement has been reached, and there are agreed mechanisms—such as references to external arbitration—to resolve the situation if negotiation fails to produce an agreement. Changes of this kind are imposed by employers very rarely indeed.

Between these two extremes, much more ambiguous situations can arise, and the inexperienced manager or authority may drift into a negotiating position when a more skilful approach would have kept the issue in the purely consultative field.

For example, several authorities have wished to introduce systems of staff appraisal. They have designed schemes and then put these to the trade unions, saying in effect: 'Do you agree to this?' The unions have obviously treated such approaches as an acceptance of a negotiating situation, and in a number of instances have rejected any form of appraisal scheme which has been put to them in this way. Accepting the negotiating stance, the authorities concerned have consequently failed to introduce any form of staff appraisal.

Other authorities have made it clear from the start that they view appraisal schemes as matters for consultation, not negotiation. As one authority put it: 'Managers should not need trade union permission before they can discuss with their own staff how well they are doing their jobs.' Taking this view, these authorities have still put their schemes to the unions but instead of saying: 'Do you agree?' have asked 'What comments would you like to make?'

One of the standard tips given in managers' training courses on negotiation is: don't negotiate if you don't have to. Union practice is understandably to widen the ambit of negotiable issues. Too narrow a view about this by managers can certainly lead to unnecessary disputes about issues on which negotiation rather than consultation is appropriate. But there is no universally agreed or standard schedule of what is negotiable and what is not. Policy and practice will probably vary between authorities, with some being willing to go much further down the negotiable track than others. The manager's task is to get this right in the particular setting of his or her authority, and that is a matter for informed judgment. The danger comes either from omitting to consider the issue until after commitments to negotiate have been made, or from giving the impression that negotiation is accepted and then making a unilateral final decision. It has to be recognised that if employees *en masse* feel strongly enough about almost any issue, they can with trade-union organisation and support, bring the whole operation of a service to a halt. Adequate information and discussion at an early stage, however, often preserves management's ability to act and prevents differences reaching the point at which confrontational negotiation becomes unavoidable.

❏ The local government machinery

Industrial relations in local government occur within a highly structured and complex set of procedures and mechanisms, and at five different levels at least:

- at national level, within the various National Joint Councils;

- at regional level, within the provincial councils;

- at authority or local level, when trade unions meet elected members and/or chief executives and chief personnel officers;

- locally, at departmental level, usually involving the chief officer of a particular service;

- locally, at workplace level (office, depot, workshop), when shop stewards meet local managers.

National level

National collective bargaining is conducted through a system of National Joint Councils (NJCs), some of which are known as JNCs (Joint Negotiating Committees). The main NJCs are for:

- APT&C staff, with UNISON as the principal trade union.

- Manual and Craft employees, with GMB, UNISON and TGWU as the main trade unions.

  Note: It is planned to combine these two NJCs in 1995–96 to form what is known as 'single table' pay bargaining for manual and non-manual staff.

- Chief officers, with FMP as the principal union.

- Chief executives, with the chief executives' own union, ALACE.

- Fire service employees, with two unions—FBU and NAFO.

Other small joint councils or committees exist for some specialist groups such as magistrates courts' staff and youth workers. Each NJC has two sides—in effect, standing committees of elected members and trade union officers. The employers' sides are nominated by the three local authority associations. The two sides do not have to be the same size, as each side has, in effect, one vote. Put another way, agreements are reached when both sides acting as corporate bodies reach an accord. This system necessitates a common view being reached within each side—often a difficult process when on the trade union side several unions may be involved; or on the employers' side in which councillors of different political persuasion have to agree a single employer viewpoint before they can put proposals to the unions.

Although the NJC system provides for a wide cross-section of authority representatives and trade unionists to be involved, this carries the disadvantage of NJCs being far too large to negotiate effectively. Each of the two major NJCs—for manual workers and APT&C staff—has a membership of over 40, and it is impossible to conduct the necessary to and fro of negotiations in meetings of this size. Detailed bargaining is therefore carried out by the LGMB secretariat and by a few leading elected members meeting informally with a similarly small group of union officials.

There has been much debate throughout the past decade about the pros and cons of national versus local pay bargaining. Some authorities have seen the national system as cumbersome and too prescriptive. They also argue that national pay agreements prevent a local authority form exercising any effective control of its single most costly item of expenditure. Others—probably the majority—support the principle of national pay negotiation provided this leaves scope for a considerable degree of local flexibility. The reasons for differing views include:

- Public sector pay has become a political issue, with the government using public sector pay restrictions as an element in its anti-inflation and pro-market policies ... Local authorities obviously vary in the extent to which they support government policy, and this colours their attitudes towards pay strategy.

- In the mid 1980s there were severe staff shortages in many south east authorities. Their view at that time was that the national pay system was failing to provide competitive salary levels and other benefits. As a result, a number of these authorities broke away from the national system and introduced their own local pay scales and improved benefits. There was also a political element in some of these decisions, with Conservative authorities giving support to central government's view that national pay bargaining was out-dated.

- CCT regulations place major strains on detailed national agreements. Inevitably, they reinforce the market approach, and labour availability and unit costs vary considerably on a regional or local basis. For example, office cleaning is one function which is subject to CCT. The national local government pay rates for office cleaners are £1 to £2 per hour above the rates paid by office cleaning contractors in many non-metropolitan locations. The national agreement, with its one specified rate for the whole country, placed authorities (and trade unions) who wished to keep office cleaning in-house in a very difficult situation.

131

With CCT being applied to an increasing range of functions, the implication for the future of national negotiations is that national agreements will have to be less detailed, less prescriptive, more of an outline or framework on which more extensive (and differing) local agreements can be built. To quote from Brian Rusbridge, then Secretary of LACSAB (prior to the LGMB's formation):

> *When employers and unions in an authority are fighting to retain work within their grasp which entails being smarter, better and more cost effective than outside contractors, woe betide us if a national agreement gets in the way. Let us make no bones about it, in that situation the casualty will be the national agreement ... There will be a place for national agreements but it will be a different place. There is no looking backwards, it has to be forwards—towards national agreements which are enabling, supportive and encouraging. If in any way they emerge as restrictive or inhibiting to local bargainers they are done for.*

Managers, therefore, will need to take even more seriously than before their role as negotiators and the need for their authorities to analyse and design the particular style and pattern of employment conditions which meets each authority's specific needs, circumstances, aims and vision.

Provincial level

The provincial machinery exists only for the manual and APT&C employee categories. It consists of a number of provincial councils which are constituted similarly to the NJCs. Unlike the NJCs, however, every local authority within each provincial area has a constitutional right to nominate at least one elected member to the relevant provincial employers' side. The trade union sides consist of a mix of lay union members who are employees of their local authorities and full-time union officers. The secretariats for the employers' sides are provided by the staff of the Regional Employers' organisations, described in Chapter 2.

Provincial councils, as joint employer/trade union bodies, have two main industrial relations functions:

- They negotiate and conclude agreements on pay and conditions of service which are supplementary to national agreements.
- They operate as appeals bodies to consider differences and disputes which individual local authorities and their local trade union officials have been unable to resolve.

The trend, so far as negotiations is concerned, is towards a much reduced provincial involvement. Indeed, some provincial councils such as the

Southern have largely ceased to produce negotiated agreements. Below national level, that is now a matter for individual local authorities. Instead, they may produce jointly agreed guidelines of good practice or advice (rather than prescription) about the interpretation of national agreements or employment legislation.

The employers' sides, however, still maintain a significant role in providing regional views to the national employers' sides about national pay bargaining. LGMB regularly consults the provincial employers on a 'sounding board' basis about proposed pay offers. The provincial complaint is frequently that the national employers' sides ignore these provincial views.

Local level

It was noted in the opening of this chapter that within the individual authority, industrial relations activities tend to occur at three levels—council, department and workplace. The formal systems which give this pattern effect vary considerably from authority to authority. The degree of elected member involvement is particularly variable.

At council level, for example, one large county has a manual workers' joint council as its top-level body, with the elected members on the personnel sub-committee as its employers' side. It has met only twice in four years, as all negotiable issues have been dealt with either in departmental joint committees or by the county personnel officer, while most consultation with unions takes place in a separate multi-union forum. In a neighbouring district council, a similarly constituted manual joint committee exists which meets monthly with quite lengthy agendas and which consequently involves elected members in a mass of detail which the county would consider to be matters for departmental managements.

Some authorities support different systems for negotiation and consultation. They argue, with their local unions' support, that while pay and conditions of service need to be dealt with only by the recognised unions for each particular employee category, consultation is often on matters such as the council's budget or employment legislation, which is of interest or concern to all categories. They therefore support council-level joint consultative committees which involve all or many of the trade unions throughout the workforce.

Thus, in several large authorities, all the trade unions across all employee categories have formed joint trade union committees to meet with elected members (assisted by the chief executives and personnel officers). Such committees include manual and APT&C employees, teachers, firefighters and craft workers. They meet to discuss any matter which concerns them all—while jealously preserving each union's individual right to negotiate on its own issues.

The formal machinery for consultation and negotiation at local level needs to be designed to suit each authority's own style, size and policies. There is no ideal or standard system for this book to promote. For many managers, though, the informal, day-to-day relationship between them and the shop stewards (or other designations for the employees' elected representatives) is the most important aspect of industrial relations.

In these contacts, attitudes and skills are more important than systems, and if one particular factor stands out, it is the need for the manager to establish his or her integrity. Trade unions and shop stewards will accept and respect a tough bargaining stance. If the answer to a request or claim has to be 'no', that will be accepted if it is given firmly and with reasons. Good relationships with unions do not depend on a soft, concessionary approach. But effective working relationships are impossible if deceit or dishonesty are suspected. To quote a national trade union official, speaking of a national employers' negotiator:

> *He can be benign, but also very determined ... He can also display 'steel teeth' as some of his colleagues are aware ... Other qualities I have most admired have been his ability to stand back from a particular situation, however fraught. This is coupled with stamina and a willingness to be persuaded by discussion. Finally, and from the point of view of his relationships the most important, his complete integrity ...*

The other important attitudinal factor is what Lord Goodman once described as 'a determination to reach agreement'. Negotiation is not about refusing to shift from an opening position: it is about exploring a disputed issue in an attempt to find common ground on which an agreed solution can be based.

It is also essential to have an adequate knowledge of the issues under joint discussion. Managers should be wary of taking up a position on a point of employment detail without first checking whether there is some requirement within employment legislation or collective agreements which may limit the scope for change. Personnel officers should be able to provide this information. Knowledge of the local constitutional position is also important. Had this particular shop steward the authority within the union system to deal with this particular issue?

As to personal skills, not every manager is a born negotiator, but all the useful skills can be developed by personal effort and through training and coaching. Four particular types of skill require attention:

- The ability to control one's emotional response to what might be perceived as provocation. It is very difficult to make constructive progress in resolving a difference between management and unions if the union position is seen as a personal attack. Emotional commitment to a single viewpoint, or to scoring debating points in argument, is no way to achieve a sound solution.

- The ability to analyse the components in an often complex situation. There may be a hidden agenda on both sides. The possibilities for a variety of interactive concessions may be considerable. Short- and long-term considerations may be in conflict. Cool, clear thinking to separate the key points from the peripheral, and to chart a way forward between obstructions, is a most valuable skill to develop.

- The ability to communicate clearly. Serious misunderstandings between managers and unions are not uncommonly caused by inadequate or imprecise communications. The manager who replies to a union complaint: 'I'm sure we'll be able to do the right thing fairly soon' may think that he or she has successfully deferred any action. The words will probably be taken by the shop steward as a firm promise to correct the complaint almost at once. Good communication in industrial relations does not require the special skills of the public relations expert. It means saying things clearly and unambiguously and giving reasons.

- Skills of interaction. Industrial relations involve intense inter-personal discussions. The effective negotiator has either the intuitive or trained ability to sense the changing mood of individuals or groups, and to adopt the appropriate behaviour to influence these dynamics. This subject is of considerable depth and complexity; books and training courses are available for the manager who needs to understand and develop inter-personal skills. One feature, though, is of particular importance in meeting with trade unions—to be an attentive and patient listener, and to stimulate discussion by asking questions rather than making statements. Statements provoke counter statements. Questions draw the other side out. Listening to the answers will often indicate the areas in which progress towards agreed solutions can be made.

QUESTIONS ABOUT YOUR OWN AUTHORITY

- Do procedures exist for regular consultation with trade unions at workplace, departmental and authority level?

- How are issues handled which are of concern to all employee groups?

- Have procedures been agreed for the handling of disputes, discipline, grievances and grading appeals?

- Is there a policy regarding the recognition of trade unions other than those which have membership of national negotiating bodies?

- Is comprehensive and accurate information available about national, provincial and local agreements?

- Is good use made of the advisory services of LGMB and the regional employers' organisation?

- Do managers receive industrial relations and negotiation training?

11

The personnel function and its contribution

KEY POINTS

- The effective personnel department is advisory, but pro-active.

- It is concerned with the strategic planning of human resources, as well as with tactical and operational issues.

- It should provide an information base and monitor the effectiveness of the authority's human resource policies.

- It operates best as a supportive internal consultancy, not as a form of executive or administrative control.

- Organisationally, the personnel function is needed as a component of the corporate management of the authority: operational personnel work is best delegated to departments.

- CCT may require the function to be sub-divided into client and contractor units.

The central theme of human resource management is that responsibility for managing staff effectively lies directly with line managers. Every manager needs to be the motivator and developer of his or her working group and this responsibility cannot be delegated to personnel specialists.

This does not imply that the personnel function is redundant, though it does require a change in traditional local government thinking about the respective roles of the line manager and personnel officer. In local government (though not in industry), personnel work has been based historically on establishment control and on the centralised administration of many employment procedures. The establishment officer had executive authority to determine a wide range of detailed personnel matters—whether a section could employ an additional typist, the designation of essential car users, authorisation of

137

extensions to sick leave and a host of similar issues. To busy line managers, whose priority is service delivery, establishment departments and regrettably many of their personnel department successors were unhelpful central control units whose main concern seemed to be the enforcement of restrictive regulations.

While some traces of this approach still exist, there has been a steady development of a different model which matches private-sector personnel practice. This is the personnel department as the provider of specialist services and the personnel officer as the authority's personnel or people-power expert. As professionals, personnel officers provide expertise in a range of techniques such as selection methods, training systems and staff appraisal, and 'own' a body of specialist knowledge about such topics as employment legislation and industrial relations. In operational terms, their role is usually described as advisory—as distinct from administrative or executive.

The specialist model, while a very considerable improvement on old-style establishment work, does have some imperfections. In particular, its emphasis on professionalism has led to personnel officers promoting schemes and techniques because they are the latest fashion in the personnel world at large, rather than because they are what is needed in a particular authority at a particular time. There is also a tendency among all professionals—not just personnel officers—to seek perfection of system or technique when the organisation's need may be for a quick, practical solution even if it has some rough edges.

Typical examples can be found in the design or selection of computerised personnel information systems. Some personnel officers, seeking to secure a system which can be guaranteed to meet every conceivable data requirement (the 100% solution), have spent years trying to evolve complex in-house systems. During this time, some urgent needs for workforce information have gone unsatisfied, while changes in projected requirements have resulted in the system specification never being completed. Other personnel officers, recognising the importance of information about key factors and trends, have bought off-the-shelf personnel software packages which quickly satisfy 90% of their authorities' workforce data requirements.

There has also been a tendency for personnel staff to adopt too passive an interpretation of their advisory role. This may be due partly to a reaction against the powerful and usually restrictive executive status of the old establishment role. The consequent emphasis on playing only a supportive part in the management process has given some personnel officers and line managers the impression that personnel officers are there just to give advice when asked. As a result, they rarely initiate ideas or proposals, waiting all the time for busy line managers to seek them out for words of wisdom, and being critical of their managerial colleagues when this does not happen.

Effective advisers see their role as highly pro-active. As experts in their specialism, they continually scan the field of managerial activity to see how their particular input might help in achieving their authority's objectives. They offer advice, sell new ideas, search out opportunities for improvement. They do not expect line managers who are experts in other professions always to be able to identify and ask for the particular assistance which the personnel function can provide.

But there is more to the personnel role than a purely advisory service to line managers. The personnel function can contribute to effective human resource management at three different levels:

- strategic;
- tactical;
- operational.

In broad terms, its activities can be grouped into five different categories:

- advisory or consultative;
- executive;
- monitoring;
- an information resource;
- administrative.

❏ A strategic function

As set out in Chapter 1, it is an essential principle of the human resources approach that resource planning should be an integral part of the whole corporate or business management process. An authority which is developing new service strategies or which is trying to define or change its culture needs to consider the human resource implications at the policy or strategic planning stage—not as a later, subsidiary factor.

The personnel function's contribution at the strategic level can be addressed on three issues:

- What implications are there for the size, quality and organisation of the workforce in the authority's objectives for its style (or culture) and services? What employment policies are needed to secure these objectives?

- What implications are there for the authority's objectives in changes in the supply, quality and cost of its human resources? What changes in these objectives may be necessary to reflect these changes?

- What employment matters require authority-wide consistency of policy and practice, and what should these policies be?

It is important to recognise the potential interaction between service policies and human resource realities. It is not just a matter of producing a service policy first and then requiring the personnel specialist to design employment policies to fit. For example, part of a social services policy in one authority to improve the quality of care for the elderly involved a doubling of its occupational therapy service in an 18-month period. Because of a national shortage of occupational therapists, this part of the policy could not be achieved. If the personnel officer had been part of the policy planning team, he or she would have been able to feed in projections of recruitment rates and training outputs, set against projected losses of existing staff, and so help the team evolve a more realistic service objective.

Planning at the strategic level is not limited to statistical forecasts of turnover and recruitment. It should include qualitative considerations about the level and type of skills required, and about necessary changes in employee attitudes, understanding and organisation. Thus a district council which set out to develop a strong entrepreneurial culture, identified at the stage of policy development the extent to which this would require major changes in the way work was organised, in its methods of employee communication, and in the development or acquisition of new skills and abilities within the workforce. Importantly, too, the personnel officer considered and advised on the industrial relations implications of all these changes, and helped to evolve the necessary strategy for maintaining sound relationships with the trade unions.

One other important aspect at the strategic level is the identification of employment matters in which consistency is needed across all departments. The employment strategies built into service plans are often specific to particular departments. But there will also be broader objectives or external pressures which bear equally on all departments and which point to a need for common employment policies. It is part of the role of the personnel function to identify these circumstances and suggest the appropriate policies.

In the words of one authority's formal definition of the role of its personnel department: 'In employment matters in which some consistency of approach is necessary or desirable across the authority (or beyond the limits of one department) policy statements shall be formulated setting out the general directions and standards which are required.'

Typically, the issues for which this kind of policy is needed include equal opportunities, salary systems, trade union recognition and consultation, staff development and appraisal, and some health and safety matters.

It is important to note that this type of policy statement defines principles and standards. It does not prescribe detailed, administrative procedures. Services or units can evolve their own procedures provided these meet the corporate standards.

❏ A tactical function

Strategy is essentially about policy evolution and broad-based planning. Both of these aspects tend towards the long term. At the tactical level, detail becomes more important and time-scales are shorter.

At this level, the personnel function is particularly concerned with the design of the procedures and action programmes which are needed to put plans and policies into effect. One authority determined as a matter of formal policy that it needed to 'raise the standard of professional and managerial staff recruited into the authority'. It went on in planning terms to say that: 'this objective will be achieved by the improvement of selection methods through the use of a comprehensive set of selection techniques including psychometric testing'. These strategic objectives then had to be converted into practical action by the personnel officer, producing an actual selection package and arranging the necessary training for those staff who were going to administer it.

Many employment practices need the framework of a procedure to ensure that policy intentions can be put into practical action in a consistent and effective manner. Thus disciplinary procedures have become universally adopted to achieve consistent standards of fairness of treatment. Grievance and appeals procedures, and procedures for dealing with a multiplicity of issues such as extensions to sick leave, the allocation of car allowances and the recording of staff appraisals are equally commonplace. All are, in effect, the tactical mechanisms for achieving policy implementation. Their design (and redesign to meet changing circumstances such as new employment legislation) is a major part of the personnel role.

While this procedural or tactical role is widely established for the fairly routine kinds of employment issues outlined in the previous paragraph, it is sometimes overlooked when newer, less conventional or less obviously people power-related policies are involved. One authority endorsed an equal opportunity policy statement in 1983 which, after setting out its intention to prevent discrimination on grounds of race, sex or disability, went on to make the bold assertion that: 'To this end, the Council will support a vigorous and comprehensive programme of action to achieve real equality of opportunity in selection, training and promotion.' Several years later, the authority took part in a survey of equal opportunity practice. One question in the survey was: 'What changes to procedure has your council made to take account of equal opportunity issues in connection with (a) job advertising, (b) selection of candidates for interview, (c) interviewing practice, (d) staff training ...' The authority's answer to all these points was 'None', a classic case of an absence of tactical action to support strategic intention.

The tactical role is not only a matter of supporting policies and long-term strategies by producing standing procedures or routines. It also involves the personnel officer working with service managers to evolve the detailed and practical action necessary to meet immediate or one-off problems or opportunities. There is a temporary overload of work in the housing benefits office. What employment action will be most effective to cope with this: Overtime? Temporary staff? Secondments from another department? There may be no policy implications, but the tactics adopted will be of significant practical importance. As with policy evolution, however, the most effective working pattern is that of a partnership between the line manager and the personnel adviser.

❏ An operational function

Personnel specialists do not only advise: in many employment procedures and practices they have an operational role. It is in this role that there has been a tendency in the past for them to undertake some duties which essentially should be the direct responsibility of line managers. It has not been unknown, for example, for some managers to expect or permit personnel officers to conduct disciplinary hearings on their behalf and—at least from the viewpoint of the employees—to decide on the resultant disciplinary action. Similarly, it has sometimes been the practice for a central personnel office to recruit and select manual and clerical staff without line-management involvement.

In both of these examples, the important leadership position of line managers has been undermined by their absence from important decisions about their employees; while there is also a considerable risk of the too separate personnel function failing to reflect the realities of managerial and service needs.

There are, though, many types of employment work which it is helpful and effective for the personnel specialist to handle operationally. Some examples are:

- In selection, the administration and interpretation of tests of various kinds; also, selection interviewing. In both cases, the personnel officer should contribute the results of tests and interviews to the total information about candidates on which line managers (or elected managers) then make the final decision.

- In industrial relations, the maintenance of informal contacts with trade union officials, and negotiating on a formal basis (in effect, using authority delegated by top management or members) when this is agreed as an effective procedural or tactical practice.

- In training, the administration of training courses and other development processes (i.e. making them happen and run efficiently); and lecturing or leading discussion groups on human resource themes.

- In employment administration, processing many of the detailed procedures, including the maintenance of adequate personnel records and statistics.

- In employee welfare, counselling employees on matters which lie outside the knowledge or professional competence of service managers.

This is not an exhaustive list, but it illustrates the types of work in which personnel specialists can contribute to the total management process by handling operationally those parts of the process for which their particular specialist knowledge and skills are directly relevant. This aspect of personnel work can also be illustrated within an examination of the five main categories of personnel activity set out at the beginning of this chapter.

❏ Advisory or consultative activity

As has been noted already, the standard managerial concept of the personnel function is an advisory activity. It has also been suggested in this chapter that this should be interpreted as a pro-active role. It is a type of activity which can exist at the strategic, tactical and operational levels.

At the strategic level, personnel officers need to be involved in the corporate considerations of chief officers' management groups if they are to be able to integrate their ideas and advice with the development of service policies and corporate strategies. At this level, too, elected members should look to personnel officers for an imaginative and effective contribution to the evolution of human resource policies—qualitative and quantitative.

At the tactical level, there has been a growing emphasis on the role of personnel specialists as internal consultants to service departments. Departments wishing to review the effectiveness of their organisation structures, or facing problems of implementation of new service strategies, commission assistance from the personnel department in much the same way as they might use external management consultants.

A police authority adopted a strategy of shifting as much of its operational decision-making as possible out of police HQ to local divisions. The chief constable recognised that the consequent changes in operational patterns of work needed to be matched by changes to the structure and working patterns of the civilian support functions. He asked the county personnel officer to supply a senior personnel specialist to lead a review team consisting of senior police officers and civilian administrators to examine what needed to be done and to produce the necessary detailed action plan. In a district council, the director of leisure services was faced with growing public complaints about the inadequate availability of some sports facilities during weekends and bank holidays. He commissioned a joint study by personnel and finance departments' staff of the issues involved and possible solutions.

In this type of consultancy and regardless of CCT, there may a choice between using the in-house service provided by the personnel department and bought-in services from outside consultants. There is no single answer as to which is best. Comparative cost is certainly one criterion—and one which the in-house service should usually win—but it is most unwise to allow this to be the overriding factor. In the long term, low-cost but poor-quality consultancy will in any event probably prove more expensive. Other factors to consider are:

- Does the assignment need a deep understanding of the authority's or department's culture, or of other service, authority or personality issues? If so, an in-house project is indicated.

- Would the subject of the study benefit from possibly unconventional ideas or from skills which occur mainly outside local government? If so, external consultants may be in a better position to inject new thinking.

- Would the involvement of external consultants help in dealing with a sensitive issue on which entrenched and differing internal views are inhibiting progress?

At the operational level, the advisory personnel role is widely accepted. A supervisor has a disciplinary problem with a member of staff. The personnel officer's advice is sought as to how to proceed. The computer division fails for the third time to fill a vacancy for a senior systems analyst and the personnel officer suggests how the job might be redefined to make it more attractive. The office services manager, involved in re-equipping the typing pool with a second-generation word-processing, needs personnel assistance in organising the operator retraining.

At all levels, the emphasis should be on partnership between the specialist and the line manager, each understanding the other's role, but with the specialist needing to see issues through the service manager's eyes. The test of personnel solutions, whether strategic tactical or operational, is the extent to which they contribute to the implementation of the authority's service objectives—not how sophisticated they are in terms of professional personnel concepts or techniques.

❏ Executive activity

Some examples of personnel officers acting in an executive capacity have already been given, e.g. negotiating with trade unions. Of course, every personnel officer has to take executive action in the management of his or her own department. In that arena, the personnel officer is a line manager. What is being examined in this chapter, however, is a wider point—executive action which implies the authority to make decisions which are binding on other managers.

Although old-style detailed establishment control has rightly been disbanded in almost all authorities, there will always be some issues on which it is appropriate for personnel specialists to act as decision-makers. The important point is that this should occur only for clearly defined reasons and in clearly defined circumstances, otherwise line-management authority will be undermined. Three examples are:

- It may be helpful to give the personnel officer authority to negotiate within agreed limits, partly because he or she should be the expert on much of the subject matter, partly to keep top management in reserve for a possible final stage.

- Most authorities consider it essential to maintain consistency of job grading across all departments. This is best done by one manager, the personnel officer, having the authoritative say and taking the necessary executive action to achieve this consistency.

- As the personnel officer should be the most knowledgeable manager about such matters as selection and training techniques, it is sensible that he or she should be allowed to make decisions about the choice of such techniques within agreed employment procedures.

❏ Monitoring

An important but sometimes overlooked activity is monitoring the effectiveness of employment policies and procedures. There may, for example, be a policy favouring internal promotion, and a procedure intended to effect this. But is it working? In the last year, what proportion of promotion vacancies were filled by internal candidates, and what were the trends? Every policy and procedure needs to be vetted for its effectiveness from time to time.

One county council, in defining the role of the personnel department, states: 'It is the responsibility of the department to obtain, and of other departments to supply, such information as may be necessary to enable the Chief Officers Management Group and the Personnel Sub-Committee to assure themselves that personnel policies are being applied with a reasonable degree of consistency across the authority.'

Some of this monitoring will be specific to particular policies, other elements will be more general and routine. Every authority, for example, should expect its personnel department to monitor:

- staff turnover and stability rates;

- age and length of service profiles;

- grade distributions;

- training volumes and costs;

- recruitment rates and costs;

- equal opportunity factors.

Monitoring of the external environment is also important. Personnel officers need to keep themselves informed about trends in labour supply, about salary movements, about the effects of demographic change (on the output of school-leavers, for example), about changes in trade union policies or organisation, employment legislation and general trends in other employers' personnel practice and standards.

❏ Information services

Lying behind much of the advisory role is the personnel function's body of specialist knowledge and information. While much of this may be held as a resource internal to the personnel department, it needs, too, to be made readily available to any service or manager who needs it. It falls into two broad categories: information internal to the authority (such as the personnel records system); and information with an external origin (such as employment legislation).

Information technology (IT), widens managerial access to personnel data. At one time, a manager who needed to know which employees were within five years of retirement and had at least 30 years' local government service would have to ask the personnel officer—and perhaps face an inquisition as to why the information was wanted. IT databases and networks now enable managers to get this information within seconds on their own desk-top terminals. In these changing circumstances, the job of the personnel function is to ensure the availability and accuracy of information in a form in which it is 'manager friendly'.

❏ Administrative activity

To some extent, administrative work might be seen as the operational end of executive activity. Just as there are some issues on which it may be necessary for the personnel officer to have executive authority to maintain council-wide consistency so, at the other end of the spectrum, there may be some activities which it is most efficient to process administratively through the personnel department. Many large authorities have conducted studies which show that there are significant financial advantages in the central personnel department processing all job advertisements. In some cases this has been taken beyond a single authority, with a consortium of neighbouring authorities using the personnel department of one as an advertising agency—recognised as such by the trade and therefore eligible for significant discounts on standard media rates.

On a very much smaller scale, most personnel departments handle at least part of the administration involved in many conditions of service procedures—though whether this is done in a central department or in service departments' own personnel units needs careful consideration.

❑ Client and contractor roles

Personnel services are included in government's plans to extend CCT across most white-collar functions, with the first contracts for some authorities due to be let in 1996. For many authorities this is resulting in a fundamental review of how the personnel function is structured. Other authorities, however, have to some extent pre-empted CCT by the earlier establishment of an internal personnel business unit, making internal charges for its services, and with its relationship with its internal customers defined in service level agreements. (Similar arrangements have been introduced quite extensively for other functions such as finance and legal services.)

The internal market, and now CCT, result in a new form of sub-division of the personnel function into client and contractor units. This in turn has shown the need to clarify other roles, and in several cases authorities have identified and redefined these roles in the following way:

- A core role, excluded from CCT, concerned with authority-wide, organisational development and with contributing to the evolution and monitoring of the authority's human resource strategies.

- A professional client role (combined with the core role), acting for the authority in the specification and purchasing of those personnel services required on a council-wide basis. This may include, for example, management development programmes and the design and updating of local pay systems. These services may be purchased from either the in-house personnel contractor or from external providers. The professional client can also commission assistance with core functions from the in-house contractor.

- A client-agent role (combined with the core and client roles), assisting service line managers identify, specify and purchase their personnel service requirements from internal or external sources.

- A contractor role—the personnel business unit which has to survive on the fees it receives for services specified and purchased by the professional client and service managers.

There is also a choice for authorities as to whether they expect the in-house contractor to compete with external providers for the provision of personnel services (i.e. CCT) or whether the in-house unit should concentrate on work for which external provision would be impracticable, using external providers to supplement, rather than compete with, the in-house contractor.

One authority in the South keeps a database of some 100 potential external sources for various specialist personnel services and in any one year lets upwards of 30 such contracts. The authority's policy is to retain a small but highly skilled internal personnel business unit to handle the basic volume of week-to-week generalist personnel work, and to use external providers for specialist functions and to meet occasional work peaks. It describes these external providers as its personnel 'associates', and considers that by this means it is able to benefit from a much wider range of skills than it could ever be able to employ on a permanent in-house basis.

Similar organisational developments and reviews of how best to provide support services are relevant to all the white-collar functions which are becoming subject to CCT. The same principles apply to all these functions, though the nature of the external market varies considerably. For example, the financial market is dominated by a small number of large financial services companies which are able to bid for large-scale contracts for major parts of authorities' finance functions. In contrast, the personnel services market consists of thousands of small, niche providers, few if any of which could bid for a comprehensive personnel contract.

❏ Organisational location

Traditionally, personnel work has been highly centralised, even in very large authorities. Since the late 1970s there has been a very marked trend towards decentralisation, with the establishment of personnel units in many service departments and a consequent shrinkage in the size (though not necessarily the impact or status) of the central department.

Surveys of various white-collar functions show that the personnel function has been decentralised to a much greater extent than either finance or legal services. An Audit Commission survey in 1991 indicated that only 30% to 40% of personnel staff in counties and metropolitain districts worked in central personnel departments (the district council figure was closer to 60%), the remainder being located within other departments. This compared with central percentages of 70%–95% for other white-collar functions.

How should personnel activities be split between the central and departmental levels? One authority describes its approach thus:

> Departments should be responsible for the general management of their own staff resources and should have the specialist and administrative capability to do so effectively. The central personnel department should be concerned primarily with those issues which affect all departments, with advising on policy formulation, providing a central resource of advice and information, monitoring the effectiveness of personnel policies, and assisting chief officers maintain the professional quality of their departmental personnel units.

There are differing views between authorities on the organisational relationship between the chief personnel officer and departmental personnel officers. In some cases, the latter remain executively responsible to the central personnel officer, but are 'out-posted' to work in departments. The trend, however, and the pattern most consistent with a human resource management philosophy, is that departmental personnel officers should be executively responsible to their service chief officers and be integral members of departmental management teams, while maintaining a functional link with the authority's chief personnel officer who acts as 'head of profession'. In that capacity, he or she ensures the professional competence of all personnel specialists, central or departmental, and looks after their individual professional career development.

At whatever level, and in whatever activity, the human resource approach encourages personnel specialists to be in with the action so that their particular knowledge and skills can contribute directly to the achievement of effective service delivery—the ultimate *raison d'être* for the very existence of local authorities.

QUESTIONS ABOUT YOUR OWN AUTHORITY

- Is the personnel function expertly knowledgeable?
- Is its advice sought widely by members and managers?
- Does it contribute to the strategic planning of the authority's human resource requirements?
- Does it monitor and report on the effectiveness of the authority's human resource policies and programmes?
- Does it initiate proposals for action to improve the effectiveness of the human resource?

- Are these initiatives relevant to the authority's corporate and service values and objectives?

- To what extent is detailed personnel administration decentralised?

- Has it been restructured for CCT?

12

The role of elected members

- Sharply focused political views imply differences of approach between authorities to some aspects of human resource management.

- Legally, each authority as a corporate body is an autonomous employer, though no individual elected member can make employment decisions.

- Authorities are bound by contract law, and by general employment legislation. Core concepts are:
  —mutual trust and confidence between employer and employee;
  —fairness, or natural justice.

- Local government legislation requires 'reasonable' employment decisions.

- At local, regional and national level, elected members involved in personnel committees, appeals bodies and in collective bargaining should act as 'the employer'
  —not as independent arbiters or intermediaries between employees and managers.

- The members' role is to ensure the authority is well managed rather than to undertake detailed managerial tasks.

- Regardless of political differences, all authorities support effectiveness, public service and the value of local government itself: these values can shape authorities' human resource policies.

Previous chapters have concentrated on the role of managers in optimising the effectiveness of the human resource. But managers do not have the ultimate responsibility for the direction and performance of local authorities: that lies with elected members. Members vary considerably in their perception of their proper role in relation to the employment of staff.

At one extreme is the view that employee management is an administrative task which senior officers are employed to handle. On this view, member involvement is minimal, being restricted in the main to the oversight of resourcing policies—particularly staff numbers and costs. At the other extreme, some members see the authority's employment style as an essential element in a much wider set of political objectives. On this view, elected members need to be closely involved in both the evolution and operation of employment policies to ensure compatibility with the aims and desired character of the authority as a whole.

Local government is a political institution, and it is inevitable that these two extremes are often described or perceived in political terms. The first view is the more traditional and places great importance on the political neutrality of officers. The second, and more directly political view is that while employees are free to hold their own individual political beliefs, authorities who wish to promote overtly socialist or 'market-right' philosophies cannot exempt from such principles their own employment policies and practices.

The effect can be seen in the Civil Service in such action as the banning of trade union membership at GCHQ, and the introduction of market-testing and performance-related pay. Changes of this kind have been initiated and driven by ministers—by politicians—not by senior Civil Service management.

In local government, similar politically driven changes in employment practice can be seen among both Labour and Conservative authorities. For example, there have been major differences of political approach to the question of national or local pay bargaining. Most Labour authorities support the continuation of influential national agreements, partly as a means of securing a more equitable or egalitarian distribution of earnings. Against this, some Conservative authorities—particularly those on the market right—are opposed to any national standardisation of wage rates and to the use of pay agreements as an instrument of social policy. In both cases, policy about pay is being treated not as an internal, politically neutral, administrative issue, but as an element in a political philosophy.

This emphasis on political extremes overlooks one other form of member involvement in employee management which is still quite common in smaller authorities. This is characterised by members making decisions about a wide range of quite minor matters. There are still some authorities, for instance, in which members conduct selection interviews for staff below managerial level, while in many others, even the most minor changes in departmental establishments have to be referred to committee. Often, this degree of detailed member involvement occurs without any articulated political or other rationale. It is just the way things have always been done. Members in such

153

authorities would do well to reconsider the extent of their involvement. They might ask, particularly, why they are employing experienced managers, and how such managers can gain the respect of their staff when they are not allowed by members to make even the simplest of decisions about, say, the selection of a new housing assistant or the payment of a telephone allowance to a peripatetic building inspector.

❏ The legal position

Whatever form the involvement of elected members takes, it needs to be recognised that it requires legal legitimacy. In this field, as in all other member activities, there is a legal base-line.

The first important point is that an elected member, as an individual councillor, has no authority whatsoever to decide any employment matter or to issue any instructions to a local government employee. Yet acting collectively, members carry all the power and responsibility of 'the employer' and have the full right, within the law, to engage, deploy and dismiss.

As was explained in Chapter 1, local authority staff are not employed under any form of national contract: each authority is at law an autonomous employer of its own staff. The employer is not the chair of the personnel sub-committee or the leader of the council—it is the council itself as a corporate body. Councils do, of course, discharge their employment functions through committees and panels, bit a panel's decision—e.g to offer an appointment to a candidate—commits the council as a body to the contractual and statutory implications of that decision.

Three different legal factors are involved:

- the common-law concept of a contract;
- general employment legislation;
- local government legislation.

The employment contract

Within common-law principles, a binding contract of employment is concluded when a verbal offer of employment is made and accepted. When a members' selection panel tells a successful candidate, 'We're pleased to tell you that we would like you to take up this appointment: will you accept?', and the candidate says 'Yes', a contract has been concluded. A panel which has second thoughts may find it an expensive business to change the decision, even though nothing has yet been put in writing.

Another important common-law concept is that an employment contract can operate only if each party—employee and employer—acts in a way which maintains mutual trust and confidence. If either party acts in such a way as to destroy that confidence, the other party is justified in treating the contract as terminated. Breach of contract, or unfair constructive dismissal may then be established with heavy financial penalties.

This legal principle is particularly relevant to the nature of the member/officer relationship at chief executive and chief officer level. Members can support or destroy senior officers' effectiveness by the extent to which they include or exclude them from discussions, or by listening to or ignoring their advice. Developing a partnership of approach between members and officers is not only a matter of sensible authority management. It is a principle supported by the legal concept of mutual obligations and fairness.

Employment obligations

Employment legislation has proliferated since the 1960s, and members need the specialist advice of their personnel officers and solicitors in keeping abreast of the implications. But although the detail of the statutes is complex, there are some general underlying principles which are helpful for members involved in employment issues to keep in mind.

Broadly speaking, statutory rights can be classified as individual or collective. The five most important rights of the individual employee are:

- not to be dismissed unfairly;
- not to be selected for redundancy unfairly;
- not to be discriminated against on grounds of race or gender;
- to be free to join or not join a trade union;
- to be provided with a safe working environment.

Much of the relevant legislation is based on the twin concepts of fairness and reasonableness. Fairness includes several principles, most derived from the common-law concept of natural justice. In particular:

- Unsatisfactory employees should be told of their faults and what improvements are needed, and given an opportunity to show improvement.

- Prior to any disciplinary action, they should be given an opportunity to provide an explanation, assisted if they wish by a trade-union representative or friend.

- Rights of appeal should be provided to the highest level.

- Employees should be treated consistently.

Reasonableness is less easy to define, but includes two basic principles:

- Conformity with generally accepted current standards of good employment practice.

- Practicability—the law does not expect an employer to adopt cripplingly expensive solutions or to abandon necessary organisational change solely because this change will affect employees detrimentally.

Collective rights apply mainly to trade unions, and legislation since 1980 has progressively restricted what trade unions can do without falling foul of the law. Four particularly important principles are:

- Trade unions have a right to be consulted about impending redundancies.

- Trade unions have legal protection when taking direct, but not secondary, industrial action—provided they have secured support for such action in a ballot.

- Closed-shop arrangements can be enforced only if supported by a ballot which has to be repeated every five years.

- Collective agreements between trade unions and employers are not themselves legally enforceable although their provisions may be incorporated in individual contracts of employment.

Local government legislation

There is very little legislation specific to employment in local government. In the main, authorities are bound only by the legal constraints which apply to all employers. The Local Government Act 1972 does, however, lay down three important principles:

- An authority may appoint such staff as it considers necessary for the discharge of its functions.

- These staff may be employed on such reasonable terms and conditions as the authority thinks fit.

- Authority to act may be delegated by a council to officers except for some specific issues (such as determining the annual budget) for which the statute requires a council or committee decision.

These principles give an authority a great deal of freedom in determining its human resourcing policies, although three important restrictions should be recognised:

- Staff can be employed only for functions which are required or permitted by statute.

- Terms and conditions must not be better than 'reasonable', the interpretation of this in any disputed case lying first with the district auditor and ultimately with the courts.

- The employment of staff for some activities is influenced by the requirement to submit these functions to the competitive tendering process.

It is worth noting that this legislation permits an authority to operate its own local system of pay and conditions. There is no statutory requirement to follow national agreements, except for teachers and police whose salaries are promulgated by statutory instruments. However, where statutory provisions exist (e.g. for redundancy compensation) it is unlawful for an authority to exceed these specified payments.

❏ Formal member involvement

In terms of formal or structured activity, members' involvement in human resource management takes eight main forms:

- personnel committees;

- selection panels;

- disciplinary and appeals panels;

- grading appeals panels;

- joint consultative and negotiating committees;

- employers' sides of provincial councils and national joint councils;

- personnel committees of the three local authority associations;

- membership of LGMB.

The last three of these categories take members outside their own authorities and into the regional and national arenas.

Personnel sub-committees

Personnel committees—or, more normally, sub-committees of policy and resources committees—provide the formal mechanism for the determination of human resource policies and for executive employment decision which are not delegated to officers. Authorities vary in the extent to which their personnel committees can decide on staffing matters independently from service committees.

The large degree of separation from service committees which exists in some authorities must raise questions about the effectiveness of their management of the human resource. If one of the main themes in Chapter 1 is accepted— the importance of integrating employment and service objectives—it is difficult to justify a convention whereby a personnel committee decides staffing and organisational structures independently of service committees.

A different approach adopted by some councils is for the personnel committee to define only common principles or standards, leaving service committees to decide their own detailed staffing levels and structures. Other authorities have gone even further, disbanding personnel committees altogether and delegating decisions about staffing levels entirely to senior management, provided the results of these decisions are kept within financial budgetary limits. In these authorities, the policy and resources committee deals with major, strategic human resource issues.

Panels

Members' selection panels have a critically important role in influencing the style and quality of top management. Selecting a chief executive or chief officer can go a long way towards making or marring an effective service, and the process is too often handled in an unskilled manner. Members should insist on the use of an array of selection methods, so that when a decision is made it can be based not just on the impression gained by a conventional panel interview, but by the results of selection tasks (such as the submission of a piece of written work), selection tests (including personality profiles) and reports from earlier short-listing.

Members' panels also become involved in dismissals, through appeals processes, and in job grading. Perhaps the most important point here is the acceptance that a panel is not acting as an independent, quasi-judicial body. It certainly has a duty to hear each case fairly, but its role is to make a final decision as the employer, not as a neutral assessor. It is not a panel function to act as a mediator between employees and management or to search for compromise solutions for their own sake. The two tests for a panel are:

- Have we considered the case fairly, having regard to the general principles of natural justice?
- What is the decision which, within these principles, will best serve or support the authority's aims and policies?

Consultation and negotiation

The same point applies to members' joint consultative and negotiating meetings with the trade unions. Councillors are often brought into the industrial relations arena only after the unions have reached deadlock with management. There is an understandable tendency for some members (particularly those with a trade union background) to react by criticising and perhaps reversing previous managerial action.

Situations may arise in which such an approach is justified but, in general, members' involvement in industrial relations is most effective when it is perceived as the final stage in a hierarchy of co-ordinated employer action. What this requires of course, is a rapport between managers and members which ensures that the stance managers take is one which is consistent with the style and objectives of the authority as set by the members.

In the consultative arena, members have a valuable role to play in explaining to the trade unions the political and economic imperatives which are shaping service and operational policies. Trade unions and staff may not always wholly agree with the members' policies and priorities, but a great deal of trouble is avoided if these aims are at least explained and understood.

Provincial and national bodies

Members who serve on these bodies bear a heavy responsibility. Their decisions will impact on many authorities apart from their own. Over the years there have been many criticisms of national agreements which fail to reflect local realities. Yet every member who participates in the provincial or national negotiating machinery has a local base. There are no 'national employers' in the real sense.

What these members need—and many, though not all, ensure they obtain—is accurate and perceptive briefing by their own chief executives and personnel officers about the impact locally of national decisions. They also need to be attuned to their authorities' employment and financial policies, and this is difficult if they are back-bench members who take little part in local policy discussions or who are not members of personnel or policy committees. There have certainly been cases in which an authority's representative on an NJC has expressed diametrically opposite views to those put forward by the authority's association member of a local authority association's personnel committee on the same topic, and in which neither view has been in accord with policy statements agreed by the authority's personnel committee.

❏ General issues

Three major questions underlie much of the detailed activity of members in human resource issues:

- Where should the line be drawn between managerial and member action?

- To what extent should employment issues be politicised?

- What can members do to achieve a highly motivated workforce?

Members and managers

In a formal sense, there is no ambiguity about the respective and different roles of managers and members. The constitutional and legal differences between an elected councillor and an employed manager are obvious. Yet in practice there can be confusion and friction between members and managers about the extent to which members should be involved in the managerial process.

Members find themselves pulled from the policy formulation role and into the implementation role for a variety of reasons. Sometimes the style of implementation is itself a policy issue. In other instances, a member may be more attracted to the practicalities of actual service delivery than to the more abstract debate of principles. Others again may be critical or impatient about the way managers are handling individual cases and will want to intervene. Apart from legal and political considerations, there are three practical reasons why members need managers to put policies into effect, and why members should be very cautious about taking over day-to-day management activities:

- Practicality. It is not possible for a small number of lay persons, most able to devote only part of their time to council affairs, actually to make all the decisions needed for the functioning of their authorities. The larger the authority, the more this is so. To consider employee selection alone, an authority employing 2,500 staff with an annual turnover of 10% will need to interview upwards of 1,500 candidates annually. Authority to select most staff has to be delegated to officers if members are not to spend most of their time in selection panels.

- Expertise. To consider only employment matters, the task of managing the human resource has become increasingly complex and requires an expert knowledge of collective agreements, employment legislation, selection and training techniques, pay and pensions regulations and a host of other matters. Trained managers, supported by expertly knowledgeable personnel specialists, are needed to handle employment processes efficiently and effectively? Members' expertise lies in their knowledge of the community and of the political process. This expertise and that of managers is different though, in a well-run authority, complementary.

- Managerial leadership. Effective human resource management requires leadership qualities to be displayed by every officer with staff management responsibilities. Leadership involves the establishment of close, effective hour-to-hour contact between managers and their staff—explaining, directing, enthusing, encouraging, monitoring. Members cannot fulfil this role, having neither the time nor locus as individuals to become the leaders of working teams. The unstructured or unpredictable intervention of members to displace or override a manager may achieve the occasional short-term benefit. If it happens frequently, however, one inevitable result is that the manager will lose credibility in the eyes of the staff, and her or his ability to lead and inspire—central to effective management—will be seriously impaired.

Politicisation

The extent of politicisation of employment policies and practices involves deeper issues. If the concepts of human resource management described in Chapter 1 are developed to the full, it might be argued that a socialist authority should develop a full-blooded socialist set of employment policies, and a Conservative-right council should likewise adopt personnel principles which strongly reinforce its political character. But doubts must be raised.

It is the essence of the democratic principle that the political complexion of an authority can be changed through the ballot box. Is it equitable or practicable to expect employees to experience fundamental changes to trade union relations, payment systems and departmental organisation every time the authority changes its politics? Further, what political characteristics should shape the employment policies of a hung authority?

These questions are not concerned just with the appointment of senior managers. Very few members support overt political appointments, though all can rightly expect officers to understand political objectives and to provide energetic, effective, supportive management. The Widdicombe Committee examined this issue and while concluding that greater recognition should be given to the essentially political nature of the institution of local government, said that officers needed to avoid political identification.

What is needed, perhaps, is an emphasis on the objectives with which all authorities would agree, regardless of their political colour. Lying behind many of the ideas in this book is just such a set of values, and these are being used by authorities with very different political beliefs to shape their service and employment policies:

- An emphasis on the three Es—economy, efficiency, effectiveness. Maximising the use of scarce resources is an objective shared by all responsible authorities.

- Public-service orientation—the recognition that services should be responsive to the needs of the 'customer'. It is a belief that can be shared by left and right in the political spectrum.

- A belief in the value of local government itself.

Setting the scene

The last point in the previous paragraph provides the clue to the answer to the question: how can members achieve a highly motivated workforce?

Members create the institutional and attitudinal environment within which all staff from the chief executive to the office cleaner have to work. A highly motivated workforce is one which understands what the organisation is trying to achieve, is enthusiastic in working towards this end, has the expertise to produce results and takes pride in its achievements. Above all, it needs a sense of purpose and recognition.

Chief executives and chief officers can go only part way towards creating this purposeful environment. If political direction is confused or inconsistent, if the member structure is driven by destructive personal or political rivalry, if members give the impression that they see only the faults among staff and never recognise effort, worth and achievement, then even the most brilliant managers will be hard-pressed to generate more than mediocre performance from their staff.

An authority's workforce is the powerhouse for the delivery of its services. Ensuring that staff are well informed, well managed, well trained, recognised for their achievements and fairly rewarded, is not a peripheral matter. It is central to realising the enormous capability and commitment which lies within the human resource. Only an authority's members can set such a scene and create an environment in which high performance becomes the norm.

QUESTIONS ABOUT YOUR OWN AUTHORITY

- What principles are followed in deciding the extent of member involvement in employment processes?

- Do members who are so involved (e.g. in staff selection) receive training in the relevant skills?

- Do members who sit on appeals or disputes panels see their role as that of an employer or as an independent assessor?

- Are members of the personnel committee well informed about the statutory and common-law principles governing employment procedures and standards?

- Do members who participate in provincial or national bodies receive regular and adequate briefing from relevant officers?

- How are these members selected?

- Do members generally perceive one of their roles as being to define the authority's values and objectives and ensure that these are communicated to the workforce?

- Are members concerned to maintain high standards and high morale among the workforce? Do they receive monitoring reports on this? Do members contribute positively to the achievement of these goals?

Index